Train Ride

to Bucharest

Poems
by Lucia Cherciu

For Karl and Madeline

Designed and typeset by The Sheep Meadow Press
Distributed by The University Press of New England

Cover image: Romanian painted monastery
Author photograph: Lucia Cherciu

Library of Congress Cataloging-in-Publication Data

Names: Cherciu, Lucia, author.
Title: Train ride to bucharest : poems / by Lucia Cherciu.
Description: Sheep Meadow Press : Rhinebeck, NY, [2017]
Identifiers: LCCN 2016048457 I ISBN 9781937679699 (pbk.)
Classification: LCC PS3603.H474 A6 2017 I DDC 811/.6--dc23
LC record available at https://lccn.loc.gov/2016048457

All inquiries and permission requests should be addressed to the publisher:

The Sheep Meadow Press
PO Box 84
Rhinebeck, NY 12514

Acknowledgments

Many thanks to the editors of the following publications in which some of these poems appeared previously:

A Shot Glass Journal, A Slant of Light: Contemporary Women Writers of the Hudson Valley, Adanna Literary Review, Allegro Magazine, Antioch Review, Ascent, Avalon Literary Review, Belletrist, Big Muddy, Bracken, Briar Cliff Review, Broadkill Review, Cape Rock, Chronogram, Circe's Lament, Connecticut Review, Edible Flowers, Eleven Eleven, Gravel Literary Magazine, Gulf Stream, Haiku Journal, Hysteria Anthology, Innisfree Poetry Journal, Interdisciplinary Studies in Literature and the Environment, Juked, Lake, Legacies: Fiction, Poetry, Drama, Nonfiction, Literary Orphans, Main Street Rag, Mudfish Review, Mud Season Review, New Millennium Writings, Off the Coast, Palimpsest, Paterson Literary Review, Poetry East, Poetry Quarterly, Pyrokinction, Respiro, Salamander, Shot Glass Journal, Sleet, South Carolina Review, Stirrin, Sweet Tree Review, Teaching English in the Two-Year College, Tinderbox Literary Journal, Tranquility Anthology, Two Cities Featured Works Blog, Undead: A Poetry Anthology of Ghouls, Ghosts, and More, Unrequited: An Anthology about Love Poems about Inanimate Objects, Vassar Review, Westchester Review

Special Thanks

With gratitude, to Stanley Moss, Greg Miller, and the rest of the team at Sheep Meadow Press. With love, to my kind friends who have shared the exuberance and camaraderie of writing: Jan Zlotnik Schmidt, Judith Saunders, Raphael Kosek, Melanie Klein, Anne Gorrick, Jeff Schneider, Jo Pitkin, Angela Hooks, Suzanne Cleary, Laura Donnelly, Vivian Shipley, Mihai Grünfeld, and Larry Carr. For the President of Dutchess Community College, Dr. Pamela Edington. Always, for Betty and Murray Ross, Deanna Speer, David Naylor, Teresa Derrickson, and for Father Alex Vinogradov. For my teachers: Cristina Mazilu, Gheorghe Zaharia, Mircea Dinutz, Ioana Gogeanu, Ioana Zirra, Susan Comfort, and Karen Dandurand. For my father, Ion, who told the best stories. For my mother, Ioana, and for Vica, Vio, and Ionuț. For Karl and Madeline, who make me laugh every day.

CONTENTS

A BUCKET OF BITTER CHERRIES

A BOUQUET OF TULIPS

FLIGHT HOME

WANDERLUST

A Bucket of Bitter Cherries

HIDING THE I

The most painful word is *I* because in my mother tongue
I is always included in the verb, implied
so I don't have to struggle all the time to hide it,
I don't have to play games like *you and I.*

Saying *I* is like wearing your sex on your forehead,
like a teacher used to say about wearing a ring
on your forefinger—saying *eu* as rare
as asking, *"Who? I?"*
Wearing a diamond ring on your tongue.

TORTURE

In the silence of stone, the teacher asked us
to stand up and recite the grinding mantra

in front of the class. Political Economy
during Communism was a jumble of quotations

from Nicolae Ceaușescu, monotonous syntax,
implacable paragraphs sprinkled with

*socialist means of production, agricultural
cooperative,* and *golden future.* Dulled

by the inertia of nouns and non-existent verbs,
we swayed softly, trying to spit back a silk thread.

Rust ate away at the core of promises.
Hope slumped under the burden of lies.

Sentences we were forced to learn by heart
flapped their wings like blind bats.

THE BUTCHER

Blistered fingers swollen
as if held under water all day,
the butcher explained that once she had to stay
in the hospital for a month from a hand infection.

What gloves? She laughed while cleaving large
hunks of meat. The man who brought the pigs
just hung them from the hooks.
She had to bribe somebody for this job,
and her husband had to intervene.
In the wide-open store, the meat
went so fast, she didn't even need refrigerators.

In the rusted-iron smell of blood,
warm breath still lingered
on cow tongues laid out next to impeccable livers,
people waited in line by the hundreds,
but she only sold bones shorn, cleaned
until they shined. The pig's whole head—
snout, eyes open, teeth, lashes, ears—
all a delicacy, as she wrapped it with bare hands
in wax paper, laid it on the scale
while flirting with a customer.

The smoked pig's feet
she saved for the pastry vendor
as they bartered. The prime pieces, for steak,
she sold under the counter to friends or party officials
who helped her get the job. The most coveted
position in town, she admitted,
holding out her hands,
nails broken, cuticles shredded,
raw ground meat.

MILK AND WINE

In a second language I don't overhear things—
eavesdrop on the rain. I don't have peripheral vision
because the center is left at home
so here is only a halo of a place with a porch elsewhere.

I don't hear whispers at night: have to read lips
to comprehend the river.

Water sounds the same way: the creeks of home
chime on ear drums, intimacy of rituals where love words
decanter like doubly distilled alcohol.

In a second language wine tastes like milk
because I was born in wine country so everyone
leaves out wine bottles on the steps at the gate—
and when I call my mother and ask her how she's doing
she says she's making wine,
bartering plum brandy for fire wood.

HOW TO MAKE YOUR MOTHER LAUGH

Even after living in a different country
for twenty years,
I read my hometown paper twice a week,
collect stories,
details about the price of milk,
and learn that you can translate salaries
internationally
in numbers of chickens.

A woman left her three children
home alone for seven days,
all between two and six years old;
when they were found
they were eating cardboard,
huddled together for heat.

A couple sold one of their children
in France for a ticket home.
A woman abandoned her four-year-old daughter
in a corner of a cemetery
in gray-black winter.

A highly-educated woman,
showed in a picture
as very attractive and trendy,
killed her mother
by suffocating her with a pillow
then hanged herself from a pipe.

Then I call my mother
and we laugh together.
She tells me
that Lelea Irina from our village
got on the bus to see her daughter
for Christmas
but somehow never arrived.

FITTING FOR NEW SOCKS

It takes a month to knit a pair of socks,
tight gauge and four thin needles:
the stitch small, the work double.
She stays up late, remembers
stories her thread reels in,
lets her cup of tea get cold.

They last for years,
reappear every winter. The art
of darning socks: a truce
with time, thoughts woven
in yarn, the way they used to make
jewelry from knitted hair.

The time it takes to repair them
mints them:
used socks, more intimate.
Afternoons snowed in,
we smirk at store-bought things.

No warmth like her hands
as she fits my feet
for a new pair,
no matter how high the thermostat,
how empty the room upstairs.

As if She Knew

for C. S. (1968-2011)

I wanted her scarves,
her earrings and diaries,
her handheld mirrors,
her hair brushes, and her shoes.

I wanted to go to her house
and clean her tea cups,
the smudge of lipstick
on the rim.

I wanted to go through her closet,
organize her camisoles by color,
even the pieces I couldn't tell
if a tube top or a skirt.

I wanted to take away her reading chair
and haul it back to my house,
place it in front of my window
and laugh her careless laugh.

I wanted to go through her jars
of make-up, stick my fingers
in some sweet-smelling goo
and spread it on my face.

I wanted to steal her sexy dresses
and wear them with high heels—
but most of all I wanted her books
that she bought with abandon
as if she knew.

STEALING THE PATTERN

At nineteen, my mother spent a winter
hunched over the loom, weaving a fifteen-foot long
tapestry, a pattern with peony bouquets.

The loom took over the room, each piece cut
by a master in the village. Everyone in the house
shuffled around, tiptoed to the table.
She worked all day, her back covered
in a sheepskin vest to keep out the snow storm
that snapped the pines, cut the power.

She sheared the wool, spun the thread,
steeped the colors. Hues melted:
subdued orange of onion skins, red of beets.

After patience and toil, flowers cropped up
on her warp and weft. After months of grind,
peonies took over the house in a winter spanning

November to May. She counted threads and days,
and after all that pain she hid the finished
tapestry for a while lest somebody steal the pattern.

Forty years later, she gave it to me, but I didn't have
walls wide enough to hang it, so I tucked it away in a closet.
Heat steeps the aroma of lovage and basil.

A river, the tapestry unfolds itself at night, floods
the room, overflows the basement, fills the house with the call
of summer. Eager for someone to steal its pattern.

DOUBLE-DISTILLED PLUM BRANDY

"We finished picking up the pears, and I keep
hiding them for you. Then I remember you're not
coming home this fall," my mother wrote, filling
the two pages of the letter front and back.
That was twenty years ago, my first year abroad,
in Colorado, away for graduate school.

My mother wrote every couple of months, described
the horse-chestnut trees and the kids going back
to school, told me that she was making red wine
and now the *must* was singing when you poured it
in a glass: still sweet yet turning, bubbling like soda,
apt to give you a headache if you drank too much.

She said she stayed all night to double-distill
the plum brandy because she didn't trust my father:
he tasted it too often to see if it was ready. She knew
how to wait, sensed the concentration of the alcohol
and didn't need to listen to the neighbors
who claimed to help, solicitous and vain.

My father wrote only one sentence in the corner,
a talisman, in his handwriting I recognized
from the lists he wrote in a blue notebook
for paying utilities, debts, and bills:
"You won't even realize how quickly
time will pass, and you'll be home again."

WASHING OUR HAIR

My grandmother combed her hair
sitting on a chair in the sun.
She washed it in lye
brewed in an old cauldron:
ashes gathered from the wood stove
and simmered till they turned into syrup.

If she didn't have time to boil lye
then she collected rain
dripping at the eaves in a vat,
or during a summer of drought she fetched water
all the way from Lelea Dochița in the valley,
balancing the buckets
on a *cobiliță* on her shoulders.

She used a bone comb
to rub in her hair petroleum
that we usually kept for lamps
and I always worried,
but I never saw a woman with her hair on fire.

Sometimes she simmered walnut leaves
to tint my bobbed hair auburn
and steeped chamomile flowers
to wash my sister's hair.

Other times she brought a fresh egg
and rubbed it into my hair,
rinsed it with apple cider vinegar till it sparkled,
and after all that work
she told me that my hair looked like hay
not golden and soft like my sister's.

THE EXPRESS

At night sometimes you find yourself on the train
with people from the past, some you haven't seen
since you were six years old, all so thrilled again
to play together. Like a child, you pick up
where you left off. Friends you haven't heard from in twenty years
are delighted to meet each other, too, even if they don't speak
the same language, but somehow they talk for hours
with an inventory of a handful of words.

Most of the time the ride is smooth, like taking the Express
from Iaşi to Bucharest, and nobody stops to check
your tickets in new stations or notice if everybody
is still alive or whether they passed away when you were fifteen.

An old woman can still hug you, lock arms with you,
teach you a prayer whose words you once tried
to memorize, but never could.

Once in a while, like the local train between Buzău
and Ploieşti, your train halts abruptly in an empty field,
travelers gazing at each other, suddenly aware
of the heat in the car, the conductor nowhere to be found.
And the passengers you summoned together hang on for a while,
looking in your eyes to see whether you know.

Sometimes they don't realize when the film
of the trip has been torn. Sometimes they linger with you,
offer you an apple, as if to say they're grateful
they got a glimpse of you even for this long.

Other times, miraculously,
the train resumes, your father sitting
in front of you. He winks, his hat cocked
a bit. He is tipsy because you are all going
to a wedding in a town he's never seen before
and people you have beckoned from different countries
resume their trip together, and you fall back asleep.

Train Ride to Bucharest

In the small train carriage
with eight seats crammed together,
a corpulent man is spreading his newspaper,
covering the people sitting next to him.
It's late July and the heat is scorching
despite the curtain someone tried to pull.
No AC, an old woman complains
of the draft, sticks some cotton balls
in her ears, pulls her scarf over her head,
and doesn't let them open a window.

She stares at his newspaper.
The two college students sitting next to her
have seen the pictures,
both put on sunglasses
and step out in the hallway.

The other four passengers are either
sleeping or indifferent.
Finally, the old woman finds her glasses
wrapped in some cloth and makes out
the spread pictures on the front cover—
a naked female model,
blond hair half shaved.

The old woman stands up, grabs her bag
and hits the man on his head,
spits in his face. The man grins,
refuses to leave the carriage,
turns the newspaper over
to other pictures, much worse.

VOLUNTEER AT THE CEAUŞESCU PALACE

The tour guide (in her early twenties,
hair styled with highlights),
says that the palace was built with volunteers
and he cringes, would like to respond,
but instead just tightens his fists
and follows the group. Stages too broad,
conference rooms bloated, candelabra
oppressive with weight.

He tries to guess the price
to heat the place, keep on the lights.
Thirty years ago: he remembers
concrete everywhere and someone screaming
at the soldiers brought to forced labor.
It took them months to tear down
the staircase steps at Ceauşescu's
order—and build them back again.

Ceilings loom large. Acrid
memories, nausea.
Marching to communist songs.
He glares at the blonde woman
and fights an urge to pull her by the hair
and tell the story as it really happened.
If he were young, he would stay
after everyone left and ask her out.

They Stole the Bell

Ring the church bell to chase away the hail,
lightening, or bad spirits.
Add to the water in which you bathe the baby
a bit of rope that pulls the bell
so everyone will listen to her voice.

Church bells announce prayer times, holiday mass,
fire outbreaks, robberies, earthquakes, war,
or someone's death—
so people gather at their gates
and cross themselves.

Tuning the bell: casting the ratio
of high-copper bronze alloy.
The sound of the bell:
the community gathers,
laughs with the living, cries for the departed,
breathes in a circle of trust.

During the war, the bells were buried
to hide them from winning armies of the day
or were melted to make canons
from the precious metal, five hundred years old.

Today, the poor steal the bells
that weigh twelve hundred pounds,
cut them overnight and take each piece
to the centers that collect old metal.
Can't the collectors tell?

Sometimes the thieves bury the bells
in the woods before getting caught.
Sometimes they hide them
when they realize they can't carry them away.
Sometimes a priest melts an ancient bell
and sells it abroad.
Some churches now install alarms
to protect the bells.

NIGHT WATCHMAN DURING COMMUNISM

The frost cut through his heavy clothes,
layers he piled up, ice sewn into his overcoat fibers,
face left unshaved for warmth.

Without a gun, all he could do was scare
somebody off. At night
people were forbidden to congregate
to walk in groups.
Others bolted when they heard
a drunk man walk their way.

Instead, he headed towards him
pulling out his club. Mostly,
he used his whistle
so the man ready to attack the sole woman
returning home from her late shift
would let her go. Knives
glistened.

The cold shredded his hands,
grated his endurance.
Those were long nights.

PROCESSION

A woman in trouble went to a crone
still in the dark of dawn
and by dusk
she walked alone.

That time, the woman's father
brought her home;
he stepped by his horse cart,
hat in hand. Her head
rested on an old tapestry
with faded dahlias.

When the whole village
attended the funeral
and paced behind the ox-drawn cart
decorated with dahlias,
why did women whisper,
untie their black scarves
and tie them back?

Nobody said anything.
In the crowd, the strained
face of the official
sent to sign communist papers,
file a report—
facial muscles chiseled
with foreboding.

WOMEN IN "TROUBLE"

Her mother had three, the last one
when the kids were in college.

Her aunt had one
when her boys were in high school:
they were twin girls.

Her neighbor had three.
Still, she kept building
additions to her house.

Her sister-in-law said
she would have kept them all
had she known
they would turn out so well.

Those were hard times,
they said, and knitted bread rolls
to take to church on special days,
counting candles to light
for the living and departed.

FOUR CHILDREN

between the ages of two and seven are left
alone for days, yet they survive, room
empty, bare mattress on the floor.

The first day, the three boys and a girl
rummage through the kitchen,
search for leftovers, scavenge
for bread. At night

they huddle, gather old blankets
on the floor. Winter
crackles, burns the line between
what's inside and out:
in the fireplace, ice.

Listless and languid,
feet blue,
the children move less,
speak less,
finagle together a snack
of cardboard.

When a neighbor
finds them, the youngest
cannot cry. House
redolent with fear.
Wafting.

Trails of dirt around their eyes,
foreheads like broken glass. Too young
to tell how long
since their mother went away.

Snow Storm with Mama Tudura

At 4:30 silence sieved night snow,
no roosters. Roofs weighed down,
eyes glued, taste of blanketed sleep.

Nobody cleared the roads. We waited
in the snow for the bus that opened the world
to the nearest town three hours away.

When it appeared far away on Dumbravă,
headlights splicing the hills, snowflakes stopped
for a second to reflect the flare for miles.

We danced to keep our feet from freezing.
Mama Tudura opened her *suman* and held me
in her coat, her brown shawl spread over us.

She asked me if I still wanted to go back to school—
or we could just walk home, and she'd stoke a fire
strong enough to thaw apple trees' armor.

We watched the rusty bus skid down the hill,
loom in the nimbus of its twenty-year stench,
threadbare tires slide. She held me

until the bus slipped down the road, and she elbowed
the other scrambling passengers, pushed a corridor
through their bundles, so I could get on.

SHE HAD IT ALL

We didn't want to go to her cabin
among hills patched with buckthorn:
no electricity, no running water,
no other houses.
It got dark early, so we blew out the candle,
didn't stay up.

In summer, she walked the two miles
to the village every day,
brought fresh milk in bottles
with a corn-cob stopper,
called at the houses of her three sons,
who had helped each other to build them.

When winter arrived, it got harder
to walk all the way from Hârtoape:
even the name showed it was tough to get there,
a road precarious for carts,
shortcuts where you had to slide
through fences, duck through wires.

And yet, she had it all. The cherry tree
to the side of the house,
her knitting by the lamp,
her prayers she whispered
as she kneeled in front of the icon,
golden sequins in the window sill,
a view of the valley, the village
close enough, far away.

HOMELESS

Saghina's house used to be
in the back of our garden,
all the way up on the hill,
where today sour cherries grow.

So she walks through the village
and stops at our neighbor's house,
watches from the yard,
imagines the view she remembers
from where her doorway was.

We don't have pictures of her old house,
don't even know when it was taken down.
If only we had maps of all the houses
that moved around our yard before.

If only we knew about the trees that walked—
some every fifty years,
some every hundred years,
and those that didn't even take root well
and got cracked by the frost.

Saghina sits on the stones
in front of our neighbor's gate
and gathers her bags close.

First, she accepts a crust of bread
spread thick with plum jam
and then when the neighbor turns
she throws it to the dog.

BLOSSOMING

She was not ugly; she was not beautiful.
Skinny, with a scarf that covered her face
as she slinked by the fence at night.

When she smiled, her left cheek revealed
or maybe hid, a birthmark. The men
who lived up on the hill knew her.

Her neighbors watched her gate,
the stealthy steps of summer, and counted
months for each of her children.

The last one, with red hair,
looked nothing like her mother
or siblings. She looked like

the Godfather who had held
candles at the wedding, the valley
blossoming with gossip and gossamer.

CONTRAPTION FOR TORTURE

Knitting sweaters on the machine
in blocks of color that clashed:
blue and red, brown and green.

Each thread took over the place,
claimed the space, strained his back.
For the pattern's sake, he had to stop,

change each needle, loop each
thread with a small-eyed hook.
Pushing the heavy handle

wrenched his shoulders,
weighed his neck. For years,
in all the pictures with latticed margins,

people posed wearing his cardigans,
every stitch a signature of his pain,
every row a curvature of his spine,

his posture hunched, knees knotted,
skeleton settled with time
like an old house.

A Bucket of Bitter Cherries

The old man went to pick black cherries, managed to fill
two buckets, but then had a hard time carrying them

back home, more than twenty-five pounds each.
He managed for a while, but when he got to the creek

he left one of them on the side of the road, in a prominent
place, for someone to find it, because there was no way

he could have climbed the steep path up on the hill
with all the cherries weighting him down. At eighty-seven

he was lucky enough to walk, he laughed to himself,
but kept turning to see the lone bucket left behind,

all the pies, the plum brandy he could add them to
for taste and color, or make wine with them, spend the day

canning preserves, as if his summer too was in that valley,
sitting on the bank of that creek.

A Veil Still Covered the Garden

When the old man came home from work, the dog
was frantic, pulled at his clothes, jerked at its chain.

He walked around the property to see what happened,
and that's when he saw, right in the corner:

it covered the back of the garden, broke the fence,
and fell over the corn, barely missed

the beehives. The workers for the power line arrived
when he wasn't home and cut down his tree

that gave the best walnuts, the ones he saved
for winter, the ones the kids who had moved to England

were still writing home about and asked him to send them.
In late August, the walnuts were on the cusp. Perfect

to split with a knife and core out the milky center,
not quite ripe, not ready to shed their husks.

Reluctance

First there were grays and lavenders,
and now her skirts are getting longer.
She isn't wearing v-necks anymore,
or sleeveless shirts.
She claims her arms are too skinny,
and a nurse said something mean
about her elbows.

Retreating somewhere
like the ocean,
her body in her view
recedes into another realm,
ebbs with the moon.

Bashful like a sixteen-year-old
shopping for clothes—
interdictions
and fears, restrictions
and internal jeers—
she won't
sit for pictures anymore.

She doesn't know
how, spooled by love,
our eyes cast back indignities of seasons
reeling in her ineffable summer.

A PRINT ABOVE THE KITCHEN SINK

Wet with colors,
bursting, opening up
like compliments, the petunias
my sister has multiplied from cuttings
cascade over her balcony
on the sixth floor.

The purple petunias alone
ease the tension,
take away the monastic look,
the postulant air of her rooms,
crumbling shelves of books,

loads of laundry dried on the line
waiting on a hot day for the implacable
torment of the iron.

Only the petunias erase the backdrop
of the buzz in the kitchen,
her carrying groceries on two buses
and up the stairs,
perfume of velvet
at she rests her back against the wall,
respite from her punitive chores,
a Georgia O'Keeffe print
above her kitchen sink.

ON EVERY GRAIN OF WHEAT

Women leave their parents' home with seeds
to carry over the mountains
so if their husbands beat them

they can hide the night out
or even ride away on a horse
and not be seen from the corn fields.

They steal seeds from their neighbors,
just a handful of beans
passed down like this for hundreds of years.

They know that seeds foresee
ailments and blessings,
hunger and feasts,

define the strength of tendrils,
ruthlessness of basil,
fire of dahlias.

Reprieve from the ire of the times,
seeds restore the balance,
seal the magic of plants.

On every grain of wheat
there is imprinted
the face of God.

FOR FATHER TUDOR MARIN

This was the church that attracted
the most women with short skirts,
a *babă* complained,
but the priest laughed and said
at least they stopped by.

The word got around that he was kind,
and many came for confession,
asked for advice or atonement,
asked him to pray for good travel,
marriage, babies, good health.

People with absurd requests came in,
and he just opened the prayer book
without judgment
and read. That was all.

That day a man stepped into the church,
maybe in his early thirties.
He asked to talk to the priest,
and although it was late and
Father Marin was about to lock the altar,
he didn't say no.

Father Marin was still wearing his *patrafir*,
preparing for his walk home.
As he had given solace to so many,
he couldn't say no to this man.
First the man asked him a question from the Bible
and then, before Father Marin could turn,
the man stabbed him,

the saints looking down at them
from the walls
in this church from 1600
built on the land of an old monastery,
where at the latest renovation
they had found dozens of graves of monks.

GUARDIANS OF THE VORONEŢ BLUE (1487)

The nuns of Voroneţ are mean:
they chase the visitors away,
resent the crowds who come to venerate
but touch with dirty hands the walls
that otherwise have withstood
four centuries of rain and snow.

Some say the famous blue was mixed
with barrels of plum brandy—
that's what made the color stay,
gave it resilience and ardor.

Others claim it is the blood
shed in the battles led
by Stephen the Great who saved
the land from the Turks
and had the monastery built

to celebrate his victory
advised by Daniil the Monk.

The nuns know better:
the fierce power of denial
and renunciation, the giving in
to arches and inner shadows,
the fusing of stenciled crowns,
the sorrow in the eyes of saints
painted in frescoes. Outside,
some fool in 1859 scratched his name
with a nail on the wall.

ONLY THE RICH HAD A WELL

to water their grass, didn't plant tomatoes,
but roses and gladiolas, not plum trees
but ornamental cherries
because the fruit littered the lawn.

My mother spent a whole week
planting potatoes and thyme,
listened to advice about placing marigolds
next to leafy greens, radishes, to repel aphids.

Six weeks later, nothing grew. Even
onions, usually easy to plant, abundant,
to give to all the extended family,
even they didn't grow. They sprouted
and withered, the leaves yellowed,

wrinkled, curved back. A worm
took over the stem and ate up
any juice left in the bulb,
the whole plant pungent and dour.

Over the fence, a young woman
sprayed the concrete-covered yard
with a hose as she sunbathed with the kids,
turned up the music, sipped cold drinks
under the willow tree.

My mother worried that people with wells
sucked up water from neighbors' gardens.
At night she listened to the pump guzzle,
frogs synchronizing,
bathing in the small pools of water next door.

PENDING SALE

Now I would like to buy back that house
after more than fifteen years, although I know

that sometimes the neighborhood makes the house,
the safety of sitting on the porch

and watching people return from church
on Sunday, the smell of slightly burned

corn mush cooked on the wood stove.
Even if I go and stay overnight

every four years, that time weighs in
with all the nights I couldn't sleep,

turned to listen to the apples falling,
a window opening in the dark,

the wind rustling in the three fir trees
at the gate—I'd like to buy it all back.

Sea Buckthorn Berries

It was the buckthorn that saved us—
      no way to turn the rambling hills
into cooperatives of production, no way to take
      the people's land, rendered useless to the party
by patches of buckthorn shrubs that inveigled
      themselves into the torn clay, gorges,
ravines, and eroded soil. The arduous roots
      kept the hill from rolling into the creek.

Unpenned, the sheep thrived on the shrubs,
      wandered in wide-spread patches.
Every year people shredded their palms trying to cut,
      contain the bushes, thorns
and silver-green leaves. Not good for marking
      property edges because the shrubs swelled
overnight, took over the shrinking corn fields,
      the pear trees, competed only with hawthorn.

Party officials sent the young to pick the berries,
      but locals hardly harvested them.
Cătina is in fact good for the skin,
      an antiaging treatment, combating stress,
and intellectual fatigue. It's good for arthritis,
      gout, and skin rashes, improves sight,
strengthens the heart, the immune system,
      has ten times the vitamin C of oranges.

Our grandmothers made wine with it,
        added it to plum brandy,
made a syrup of buckthorn and honey.
        Then we didn't know. Today, my mother
makes me juices, jams, and jellies
        to treat colds and allergies, make my skin
glow, hair shine, heal departure and displacement,
        cuts and wounds.

Previous Owners

They left for us daffodils
she planted around the yard
beside hyacinths, snowdrops and crocuses.
When they went hiking, they brought back
wild ginger. The yellow lady slippers
came from her aunt, the painted trilliums from God.
She bought perennials from expensive stores
and left us catalogues with glossy pictures.
She scoured old books and made copies of pages
describing the rarest flowers in the garden.

Out of red oak from a barn in Vermont
where his grandfather used to live,
her husband made a royal-looking chair
that reigned over the backyard.
Bird houses fashioned like a school
and a church hosted new guests come spring.

And thirty years ago, after one of their twin boys
just twenty years old died in a car accident,
they spent even more time in the garden,
tending the ancient lilac,
mulching the ferns,
weeding the basil, thinning the blue bells.

LINDEN TEA

I found every linden tree in town
like discovering coffee or good bread.
Some days I take a detour
just for a glimpse.

I wait every year for the end of June
when its flowers attract thousands of bees
even in these times
when they seem to be disappearing.

Sometimes I drive to a parking lot
just to see a linden tree,
remembering the scalloped leaves
and the yellow flowers
that fill with romance
the boulevards in Bucharest.

I worship in the chapels
of linden trees. Even if I cannot stop
and saunter in, light a candle,
take in the ceilings and breathe in the awe,
I cross myself—just thinking of the flowers'
candelabras, the spicy smell.

Linden takes care of colds and sleep,
brings calm and peace—
its flowers in the cup like water lilies—
but mostly it keeps away
the loneliness of nobody here having tasted it.

Sipping *flori de tei* with honey
on the porch: solitude of initiation,
like being the only one who knows
that apples are good to eat.

PICKLED PEPPERS

The recipe calls for peppers,
celeriac root, horseradish, mustard seeds,
bay leaf, peppercorns, sugar, salt,
but also small twigs from a sour cherry tree.
Now if you were back home
you would just step into the garden to get the twigs,
but here it's a game of patience.

Look through catalogues for months
to find the perfect kind of sour cherry tree
and order two, plant them in the front yard,
build a fence around each of them so deer don't get them
and then wait four to five years
until they start to bear fruit.

Look through catalogues again for months
for *ardei gogoşari*—don't be fooled,
they are not regular red bell peppers:
round and flat, so dense
you'll find yourself hard pressed to take the seeds out
because the inside is all meat. Of course,
you know the difficult part will be to refrain
from just eating them with a bit of salt,
before you get to pickling them.

But you're not at that stage yet.
Plant the pepper seeds indoors in February,
buy the special light bulbs
and if you're lucky, they will germinate,
the frail shoots won't wilt in three days,
and sticky aphids won't devour them.

Or simply call your mom,
ask her a dozen questions,
entice her to tell stories about how you should place
the handle of three forks or spoons
under the jar when you pour in the boiling water—
and listen to her until you forget about pickling peppers
and the early January day warms up.

AMARYLLIS

I didn't know you were supposed
to give your amaryllis a rest.
I watered it for seven years straight,
changed the dirt once,
moved it to a bigger pot
only to learn now
that it likes smaller, snug pots.

The flowers, thriving,
are like a heart of deprivation
and endurance, blossoming
in the middle of the cold,
pulsating with the rhythm of frost
and rebirth, a test of faith.

IT TOOK THREE DAYS

At the intersection
between Innis and the Arterial
where houses ride on top of each other
and cars pile up on the curve of the sloped road
in the sleet after the snow storm,

a man was perched high up in a tree
hanging from a complicated harness
backed by three layers of insurance.

The tree loomed tall stuck between power lines,
magnificent, planted two centuries ago,
and the drivers waiting for the light to change
watched as the man sawed it off
one small segment at a time, round and smooth,
chairs in some imaginary Table of Silence,
the pieces adding up around the trunk,
a sculpture of pain
limb by limb
circle by circle
the tree still standing
day after day,
the man in his straps
lowered slowly,
planning the excavation of roots
digging into the mirror
of the crown lording over
the neighborhood.

SPRING IN A SECOND LANGUAGE

In a second language, every walk becomes
a lesson in botany; maple trees
speak a dialect I do not understand.
I cannot tell which leaves are good for tea,
which for soothing insomnia. I do not know
which flowers give vivid dreams and which petals
to put under my pillow in order to see the man
in my life. Back home I can pick linden tree blossoms,
dry them carefully in the shade and save them for winter,

for resplendent tea. I can cure
a cold with horseradish. I recognize the birds
by their song, let them make a nest on my porch.
Here, the trees don't whisper to me,
and my own grandmother
hasn't passed down the stories about how deep
their roots burrow under the foundation of the house,
displacing it if planted too close. Here
I don't know how to protect the new tulips.
The deer come and steal my herbs
I have carefully planted. In vain
do I check books to learn the history of the valley,
the brackish rhythm of the river, the power to read in your palm
my future, my health, the promise of spring.

WALKING ON THE HIGHWAY

Since the dark, rented apartment
hid among sprawling, distended houses,
with the sun cutting the fat of the afternoon,
I headed to the highway,
the cars swishing by,
small sedans stuck between two trucks
with screeching, faulty brakes:
hours overextended,
endurance stretched thin,
gas running low.

Gritting sand in my teeth, gnawing at the tooth
enamel, I leaned forward against the speed;
despite the signs against littering,
I loitered, spotting
cigarette stubs, beer bottles,
discarded cardigans, soiled

socks, defective
sunglasses, used
condoms, calcified
wads of chewing gum.

While cars rushed by, waves of the ocean,
drivers stared me down from the height
of their indecent, guzzling four-wheelers,
wondering maybe if I had broken down,
as I braced against traffic,
trespassing in someone else's
starchy nightmare.

SPRING FRETTING

The first warm day when leaves burst
their cocoons with green, plied buds,
pickups zoom out on the arterial
like oversized June bugs caught in the wires
of the ant hill, carried on the shoulders
of hundreds of red-black dots with hairy
worming, electric restlessness,

even the sluggish, bald neighbor
digs out a rusted rake from the garage,
gathers putrid leaves
from several years, after only five yards
chokes, halts, turns back to the house,
rummages through the fridge, lights a cigarette
and collapses in a wicker chair, taking a long
swig from his cold 10 AM beer.

Meanwhile, the man across the street wakes up
and goes out for a stroll in a black overcoat,
his antennae flickering fast

between the corners of the street, caught
between two corrugated walls, whistling
softly at the mere glimpse of a light pink
camisole, polka dot flip flops,

lingers in front of the gas station,
hacks a persistent phlegm, spits
on the pavement, spreads it with the heel
of his torn shoe smudging it, careful
not to step into the dried-up carcass
of a squirrel flattened, brittle, paper thin,
the delicate smell of spring folded in
the spicy, satiating whiff of gasoline.

FEAR

Rain over snow: God
holds in armor eight pine trees
straight above my house.

EXCUSES

A three-day storm, excuses had settled around the house:
first he waited for the snow to stop to clear the driveway.
Then when he tried, the snow blower heaved under the weight
of the heavy snow, shook, screeched, and stopped.

The second day he took out a shovel and bent under the heft,
hurt his back and had to return to the house,
couldn't get out of bed. By the time the storm stopped
he couldn't open the door: snow high as the eaves.

He pulled the snow inside the living room all the way to the couch
just to open the way to the steps, then he lifted himself
by holding on to the eaves, broke the gutters, and that's when he saw
the gash in the roof, understanding now the noise upstairs

overnight, the layers of anxiety and procrastination (a word itself,
rusted and painful, the last sound in his snow blower
giving out). Excuses crusted the frame of the house, encased.
Helpless, I was a frozen film of flowers and feathers.

THEY DROVE FOR TWENTY HOURS
TO CLEAN UP THE HOUSE

Porous, the room accumulated
piles from closets to tops of beds,
sheer mix of empty bags, carton boxes,
and one-use gadgets: juicers
with remnants of fruit peel stuck in the blades,
a film covering the stove and fridge shelves
like jelly. The dead weight
of unwanted gifts, the impulse buys at the dollar store.

Cheap jewelry glittered
like theater props in a treasure trunk:
he didn't have the heart
to throw it out himself, so now his daughters
had to go through it all twice. They ordered
a garbage bin and then filled three,
couldn't save the half-dead plants, sticky
with dust. Most fixtures falling apart,
too old to give to Goodwill, shoes
stretched out of shape, folded back
like an accordion.

They tackled letters and diary notebooks:
after reading full pages
of missed deadlines and dentist bills,
they burned them in the backyard.
By the third day they were ready
to paint. In November, leaves gone,
rain seeped over clogged gutters.

AT NIGHT THE APPLES AT THE STORE KNOW BETTER

Insomnia so deep you decide to go grocery shopping.
You might better buy spaghetti rather than force

sleep. The ghosts push their carts along the aisles,
delight at the sight of grapefruit, and start peeling one,

hoping that the smell will wake you up. Remembering
the first time you entered an American store in Colorado

twenty years ago, you take in the aisles of cereal,
the hundred brands of cookies, and know that brand names

don't care what food does to you: they just try
to get you addicted. That's all they're after. They strive

to hook you, make you open a box of chocolate mint cookies
and finish it. To get your attention, the ghosts pick up a mango

and start eating it without peeling it first, and all you want
is to steal some cherries that cost seven dollars a pound.

REVISION

Like folding a fitted sheet, revision
balks at effort, doesn't

yield to zest and drive. It flaunts its bulky
seams, conspicuous.

Following instructions—even more
redundant and pointless:

place underneath, tuck corners,
slide your hand,

straighten edges. Stashed
on the shelf, it deflates

and pouts, hides its ghosts. Wistful
anamorphosis,

revision longs for the sparkle
of a magic angle.

TRANSLATING MY OWN POEMS

is as absurd as taking the trouble,
building the euphoria to pay for the parking fee,
board the train, travel for two hours to the city,
enjoying the view of the Hudson,

only, when I arrive,
instead of getting off at Grand Central
and joining the crowd slick in black,
find out immediately when the next train returns

and maybe, if I am lucky,
even discover that I can simply wait
on the same train,
and just come back to Poughkeepsie,

rather than straighten my tight skirt,
practice my strut,
the city waiting for me at the gate, giddy, gallant.

THE NEW EDITION

The old anthology had onion skin pages
and the corner where she spilled her coffee
had sopped it up.
She made notes in the margins
in her chicken scratch
scrawled with her left hand
between the lines
and then like a palimpsest
between her own lines too.

Every time she taught "Bartleby"
she added more notes
sometimes in a different color.
She drew arrows to the few blank spaces,
scribbled three synonyms for the long words
the lawyer in the story relished:
crunchy, polysyllabic, Latinate words.

I expected her
to reread the story each time
she taught it,
crumbs of ginger snaps stuck
between pages.

What I didn't expect when I stopped by
on a sweltry afternoon
was to find her carefully copying
each word of her own marginalia
into the new edition:
"Everyman," "symbol," "metaphor."

INFINITE VERBS

Except verbs,
everything else
is sleep of vowels,
fretting of chimes.

Doubt sifts the sky like snow,
brings in silence
of Gregorian songs,
syntax of prayer
we can't translate.
We wonder if this
is what we want:
postponed fear,
elusive bread.

We latch the door,
try to keep out cursing words,
and patch the gaps
with adjectives
and cups of tea.

The only thing we have is verbs;
everything else is squandered summer
running through our fingers
as we brace ourselves

for the sundry sounds of cold,
emptiness crackling
in the gaping stove.

ORIENTATION

He used words like *robust, timeline,*
roadmaps, and *concrete,*

while the audience
meditated and prayed,

sifted his empty syllables
of bragging and pretending,

rooster-prancing
and posturing. Façade.

Time settled
like dust on lard.

They shrank into themselves,
dug deep

like the men paid to burrow
a well on the property

and after weeks of drilling
sighed in belief and disbelief.

TASTY WORDS

On the first day I asked my students
to write a list of words they loved,
maybe the rhythm, the sound,
something they cherished,
to write succulent words
and tell me why they fancy them.

They liked *monotonous, extravagant,*
flabbergasted, agitated, adorable,
pillow, blanket, flannel, warmth,
promise, and *cryptic*. A student liked
glacier and *aurora borealis*.
Another liked *mitosis* and *Fallopian tubes*.

When saying *miracle, chair, cash,*
calm and content, goof, hence,
the temperature in the room went up,
the air suddenly redolent with their
enthusiasm, their faces turning into
the colors of being in the zone,

the flow of their ink on the page,
the steady press of the pen,
pushing, scratching the page,
the fever of their pleasure
as they spelled *likewise, empower, titter*.

INEDIBLE WORDS

The second day of class I asked my students
to write down all the words they avoided
and tell me why. They didn't like

perturbed, psoriasis, and *pretentious,*
regal, allegory, and *ambidextrous,*
preface, rehearse, and *titties.*

Some said the words they disliked
they misspelled, or the other way around.
The sounds of *moist, Monday*
mundane, honey, necessary, and *cheat*
made them cringe, grated their ears.

When sharing, they were pushing back
their chairs as if trying to get away
from each other, the space too stuffy.
Crammed together in the lab,
they spoke up to cover the sound
of the computers' fans, to drown out
the syllables that offended their ears.

Words like *relax, conspiracy,*
propaganda, silence, beginning,
and *failure* rubbed them the wrong way.
They couldn't stand the sound
of *lose, can't, slice, nooks and crannies,*
sorry, pissy, reminiscence,
and *tchotchkes.* For extra credit,

I asked them to write down words
they thought I wouldn't know,
maybe jargon and argot, slang,
words nobody would tell me
words kept away from me, or maybe
I had overheard many times
but never quite understood.

THE WOMEN AT THE MET

In "The Storm" by Pierre-Auguste Cot,
the couple is running from the rain, symmetry

of bodies, legs in sync, the woman
barely clothed, the veil more alluring

than nakedness. He stares at her,
holds her cinched waist. I stare

at the dressed-up women who stroll
around the corners of the museum.

Some wear fur like the décor
in still life paintings; some sport their scarves

even better than the one-hundred-dollar silk
made in China to look like Tiffany's

on display at the gift shop. Their high heels
an imputation on the hard floors

in the marble rooms. Dazed, I rest
on the carefully nestled chair in the middle

and admire the audacity of the outfits
nobody else would wear, nowhere else

would fit: corsage and corset,
everything too tight, brimming over.

Makeup thick, hair crimped,
half curled, half straightened out,

bangs stiff with maximum-hold spray,
the paintings dimmed, fading away.

Days of not Writing

Haven't prayed for so
long, I forget even how
to open the door.

A Gardenia for My Mother

I moved all the houseplants upstairs
so they could get more sun
from the south window
and forgot to water them for days.

I bought a gardenia for my mother,
and when she left after a three-month stay
I had a hard time keeping the blossoms
from falling.

One morning she told me she thought
I had come and rested next to her—
the gardenia smelled too strong
steeped in milky sleep.

She said she made room for me in her bed
and I lay down next to her
warming her back. Not
knowing and not knowing.

MY MOTHER DREAMS

My mother dreams that she's driving a car
and takes off on a cool afternoon,
speeds for three hours all the way
to the mountains, mashes the gas pedal
with her high-heeled shoes
she bought when we were kids.

My mother dreams that she's riding a bike
and whizzes down the hill,
no brakes, no handle bars,
although she has never tried
and probably with her hip surgery
it's not a good time to learn now.

On the phone, I promise her
that when she arrives we'll take the car out
to an empty parking lot, roll down
the windows, and I'll teach her to drive,
her face glowing in the wind,
her hair blowing out of its pins.

My mother dreams that she's running
although her walking is not very steady
and sometimes when she crosses the street
the drivers try to get her to hurry,
but she says she couldn't run even if
someone were chasing her with a gun.

My mother is flying over the ocean
and worries she might get lost
during the layover, while changing planes,
prays that her papers be right,
that no customs officers ask her anything
for she can only say *hello* and *goodbye*.

AMERICAN WOMAN

A briefcase, the court files,
the breast pump,
four six-ounce bottles,
two icepacks, a steaming bag,
five individually wrapped nursing pads
an extra crispy white shirt in the trunk
in case of leaking.

*

The breast pump advertised for its best feature:
hands free, so she can pump while vacuuming,
pump at work on conference call,
pump on the half-an-hour drive
to an appointment with a business client.
Silent and discreet,
so nobody can see it,
nobody can talk about it.

*

Getting up at 3 AM to pump,
worrying the baby might wake up again
and see she has stolen his milk
to add to her stash in the freezer
in case her boss catches her pumping at work
in case she has to do overtime
in case she gets caught in traffic.

*

She locks the door to her office, the map
strategically covering the small glass window,
and sets up the pump

while responding to company e-mail,
a colleague on standby next door
in case of unexpected visitors.

*

After waking up every night at three AM to pump
in addition to the night feedings,
the freezer stacked with individually portioned bags of milk,
the test confirms that the baby's crusting rash on his face
is caused by eggs
and she donates the frozen milk—
all the sixty bags—to another mother,
and then progressively takes out different types of foods
from her own diet: eggs, dairy, gluten, citrus,
strawberries, processed food.

A Bouquet of Tulips

Only Two Minutes from Our House

Some stories say Chicory refused
to give a glass of water to a thirsty old man
so she was turned into a flower.

Others say her fiancé died in the war
and she was left behind
to cry on the side of the road.

She was in love with a sailor
who didn't return,
so every day she waited for him.

One morning the Chicory fairy
was bathing in dew when the sun
saw her and fell in love.

He sent the morning star to propose
on his behalf, but she rejected him,
so the sun turned her into a flower.

Others say you can unlock a treasure trunk
with a thread of chicory,
blue petals cutting gold.

We drank it during Ceauşescu's time
in adulterated coffee, yet now
we find out it's good for us.

Its hypnotic flowers
hold the gaze, a spiral
of meditation and prayer.

Luxuriant chicory was growing
like an eye of water and sky
that opened to the final mystery

where they found my father
on the side of the road.

In This World, May It Be for Your Soul

"Pe lumea asta să fie de sufletul tău;
pe lumea cealaltă să fie de sufletul lui..."

"In this world, may it be for your soul;
in the other world, may it be for my father's soul,"

so they say three times when they give away
a live chicken, ceramic plates, wooden spoons.

Any gift can be sent directly to someone
in the other world, no matter the size,

like some magical form of UPS,
and both the messenger and the receiver

get to enjoy it: no wrapping, no ribbons,
no card, no address.

Today it can be a shirt in his favorite color
to give to an orphan in church.

Tomorrow, bake for him
some of that flat bread he liked,

and give it to that widower with no children,
who walks in the sunset, and remember to say

the name out loud, while you both hold
on to the warm loaf, and like signing,

the old man replies, sealing the gift,
"*Să fie primit*": "May it be received."

NETTLES

My father returns from the farmers' market
and tells me to wash the nettles for soup.
I ignore him, and just one hour later
I walk into the kitchen.
On the table he has spread the nettles
that are waiting unaffected.

Among the leaves, a tulip
he has brought for me
as an offering because I went
to the national *olimpiadă* for literature.
He doesn't say so.

I pick the nettles,
shake them, tear the ends,
check them for straw and grit,
wash them in a large pot.
In the water, they wake up,
prickle, and sting. They smell
like iron and spring.

The tulip is bursting,
petals cool to the touch
folded tight
half green, half yellow.
I am sixteen.

THE TRAIN

At dawn, frost has caked the house, and my father
shovels the snow off the front steps. In the dark,

my breath ices the scarf as he pulls the sled
through empty streets. At the town's outskirts,

he walks to the train tracks, takes out an ax,
tells me to stand watch, touches the trees,

listens to them. No one around to hear
the heave of his breath. He tells me to step back

as the tree falls. Snow sifts in a cloud,
takes down the sky like a table cloth.

The tree stretches out, flat as a vein and artery
chart. Just then we hear the whistle of a train

speeding by, and I shun the passengers' gaze
as we load the wood on the sled.

NO LISTENING

He had a gift for stories, but nobody
listened, not his family. Drunkards

lingered and pressed him to stay. Delayed
after work, he arrived out of breath,

worried what she'd say. Her words
undressed any remaining enthusiasm,

spread like mold, thickened the air
in the room. Doubts and suspicions. Nothing

helped to diffuse the viscous silence.
Nowhere to escape but more of the same,

evasions and fumes of wine and loneliness,
her perpetual need for probing and prodding.

Nocturnal nodding, qualms of regret.
No easing or quickening, no leavening.

TACT

Sometimes when he told us a story, he used to hedge
his pronouns and leave us guessing, a mixture

of tact and reticence. Evasive or uneasy, he blurred
the lines so it was hard to say whom he was talking about

when telling the story of a couple making love outdoors
who were unaware that the workers in the sunflower fields

saw them, laughed, and whistled. But he forgot to say
who they were. Maybe he was protecting them;

maybe they were long dead and he brought them back
on that scorching summer day when their juices

cooled the afternoon with their manna and refreshed
the worn-out workers who paused for a moment,

pushed back their hats, and, despite the one hundred
degrees, savored the sweetness of the shade.

LETTING GO

The sour cherry tree that grew in the garden
and brought some breeze on parched days,

the tree her mother climbed to pick cherries
to make pies, syrup, and jars of *dulceață*,

the tree that ripened early, that had
the largest fruit (turned red-black),

that birds didn't bother, the one the neighbors
inquired about for soup, the tree kids foraged

for twin stems to wear over the ears,
she read her books in its shade.

Cherries were still ripening on the top
of the tree and winked safely out of reach

the bright morning after she left,
when her father axed it down.

THREE KILOS OF NAILS

Before we said goodbye, we went to the market
where he bought the cassette player he wanted,

one with a radio, which was his favorite part,
to listen to the news on long afternoons alone.

Then he needed some nails for the house
he was building slowly by himself. So we walked

around and he looked at different kinds, and after
maybe half an hour he bought three kilos of nails,

just the size he was searching for. So much work
he had already done on the house, so much more

yet to be done. When it was time to leave,
he just turned away. He didn't say much.

A couple of years before I would come back—
he avoided my eyes as if he knew more.

He Gave His Eighty-four-year-old Father a Haircut

The son told a story, tried to distract him,
paced back and forth to make sure the trim was even.

Bemused, the old man kept quiet, looked up,
wondered when they'd let him go home.

His three sons lived in different towns
and each took him for three months at a time,

then passed him off to the next. The old man
would have liked to stay in his own home

but was getting too frail. Sometime he escaped,
and neighbors came to ring at the door

to say they found him strolling in a park.
Finished, the son showed him a mirror.

The old man took to walking around with a hanky
laid out flat on his head to hide his haircut.

BOOKMARKS

When I moved to my studio in the basement,
I put my rent money in a book, promptly forgot it,

and didn't find it again. The stray things
I used as bookmarks over the years languished

forgotten on shelves dusted with care:
love notes, receipts, lists of words I collected

or looked up seven times. Meanwhile, my father
placed in his prayer book an invoice from a bank

that mounted a national pyramid scheme
right after the revolution. Everyone he knew

bragged of selling a house in the mountains
contributed to it, and won a fortune.

Although it wasn't as much money as others
had risked, he lost it all when the scheme crashed.

LEARNING A NAME

When I was a child, my father used to ask me
the name of everyone we met, and when I failed

to remember, he was disappointed and he'd say
that I took after my mother. Later, I learned

that learning a name traces a ritual like stencil
on light, repetition of gestures that matter.

Soul and breath. Sacred as rhyme in a prayer,
naming builds a ladder of salt, soothes sobbing.

Like walking on the same trail, abates fear
and restlessness: every step, a salutation

of a tree whose name I finally discover as if
its wood and leaf burn me. To a weary traveler

walking at dusk, having learned a name will offer a ride
on a deserted road even before having to ask.

DON'T ACCEPT ALL THE DOLLS THAT FIND THEIR WAY INTO THE HOUSE

Its limbs are held together on the inside with elastic
so all the parts wobble. The head buckles.

Seven pins are tucked in its hair to keep the hat on
and you worry what hides on the inside,

what holds the eyes in place and might come undone.
Your daughter likes it, despite the dirty dress

viscous with dust and grime. The doll's hair falls off,
and you know there must be ways to fix it.

Who carried such a large doll in a suitcase
over the ocean? It stares at you

when everybody else in the house sleeps.
You want to throw it out, but instead

you hide it in the attic and close the door,
fight off the memories of another doll.

Your father brought one for your sister
when she was six, you four, and all the kids

ran down the hill ahead of him to tell
about the gift. It had short red hair

with soft curls, a green polyester dress
with a white bodice. Its name was Natasha.

So what if your father brought it for your sister?
So what if there were no other dolls around?

When nobody was watching,
you combed your fingers through its hair.

A BOUQUET OF TULIPS

When my brother was born, my father took us out of school
to go to the hospital and see the baby.
My father had a bouquet of red tulips, but he asked me
to put them in my school satchel. He was drunk—
also with happiness—to have a boy again
(there had been another boy between my sister and me,
but he had died in his sleep as a baby, two months old).

When we arrived at the hospital, the nurses yelled
at my father that the visiting hours were over. No, the father
could not be present at the birth in those days.
He couldn't even see the baby later that day.
We weren't allowed to visit my mother either.

That's how things were: often we remember what we were not
allowed to do, as if those days still linger. Those tulips
stayed hidden in my bag. Today, my brother laughs
with my mother and says that he was worth the wait, asks
if we ever took out the tulips and put them in a vase.

EYESIGHT

Father says your eyesight is like a horse cart
loaded with firewood. If you use it, you run out.

How many hours, how many days, do I unload
those logs in my eyes, do I burn the light?

Screens I was not meant to read, night hours
I devoured page after page when I couldn't sleep,

moments I dallied, wasted away. He would
shudder, throw the books away. He would

send my mother to check if I'm sleeping
or reading in bed. The pleasures of life:

I am glued to a story, ensconced in a soft
light like a cocoon, but Mother cannot see me

from next door. Short on wood, today I save
for a long winter from September to May.

My Father's Trees

One year I sent back home to Romania some broccoli seeds,
and my father planted them in the garden. He didn't know

what broccoli looked like, didn't save the paper packet
with the picture, didn't know when to pick them.

He waited too long, left them on until they flowered
like a broom, and that was it. He could tell something

had gone wrong, but it was too late. At night,
he opened the window near the garden and listened

to the broccoli as it grew into a tree, transformed
and reached out all the way across the world.

He imagined he'd be able to come to visit someday.
It seemed unnatural to learn of new plants from me

when he had introduced me to the austerity of his garden
without water. He didn't harvest the broccoli that year,

and I didn't send him seeds for it again, but every time
I ate it I listened to a broccoli tree that grew in his yard.

I Wanted to Comb My Fingers through His Hair

At night we walked through the park
to replace each other—
we weren't supposed
to leave him alone in church.

Most of us tried to make sure
there were two of us at a time
not just to talk
but so we could not realize.

His brothers came.
He was the youngest.
The middle one stepped outside
to smoke, hiding so we couldn't see.

Most of the women stayed home
to cook *sarmale* for a hundred
but I hadn't seen him for a year
and I wanted to sit by him.

In church, the air felt heavy
as if I were swimming
in a cold river
and my clothes weighed me down.

It was as if I were dreaming,
and in my dream I knew
how to swim, but the truth was
that I didn't.

I wanted to reach my hand
and comb his hair,
but I didn't want
to make his brothers cry,

I didn't want to unsettle
the saints on the walls,
the faded blue folds of their mantels,
the glow of their aura fluttering.

Horse Chestnuts in Bloom

When we got home
I wrapped myself in his şubă,
his overcoat, and curled up on the bed
like a fetus and tried to sleep.

The coat smelled like him.
He kept it for best,
didn't wear it on his job,
on the milk truck
from two AM till noon,
delivering milk to all the stores in town,
lifting the crates on and off the ramp.

I left the lights on,
the way somebody said
we were supposed to do for forty days.

Outside it was already warm.
The first week in May
the horse chestnuts were blooming,
their candelabras reaching
close to the balcony
on the fifth floor,
flowers splurging
too late or too soon.

Returning Alone

Fresh apricots picked the night before
left on the kitchen table for her,

his hat left on the rack by the door
and the plates left to dry on the counter.

The pillow where he had slept
still smelled like basil and sweat.

Under the table cloth, enough cash
to buy a new bicycle for a child.

Under the linden tree in the shade, the chairs
where he had lunch with a friend.

Although it hadn't eaten the whole day,
the dog leaped in the chain, escaped,

and ran away to the back of the garden
when it saw my mother returning alone.

THE SOUL WAS THIRSTY

They paid a woman to water my father's grave
for forty days. She filled two buckets,

walked to the cemetery every morning,
and lit candles at the grave. She didn't know

my father, so she just looked at the picture,
crossed herself, checked off on her list. The soul

was thirsty and needed some water to wait out
the time before ascent. Roses had already started

to open and some teenagers came in and picked them
to sell at the farmers' market. Defiant, the flowers

fought for space. Uneasy, the woman
was afraid to confront the petty thieves

even when they stole the wrought iron bars
of the fence to sell for scrap metal.

TELLING A STORY WITH GESTURES

Can you hear? Does it bother you
when I open the door?

How do you feel
when I write again?

I can try to be good,
go outside and listen to the birds,

carry a bucket of water to the plum trees,
weed the dahlias and prop them up,

trade for some orange tulip bulbs,
variegated, to light up the garden.

Can you hear? Can you smell
the lilies of the valley?

Can you travel across the ocean?
Are you afraid of flying?

We can play chess
on our flight home, order a bottle

of red wine as you try
to tell a story to the man

sitting next to us although clearly
he doesn't speak Romanian.

MY FATHER IS TALKING TO KAREN

My dissertation director explains to my father
who Emily Dickinson was
and recites lines from memory
and my father responds with stanzas
in Romanian, from Mihai Eminescu.

Karen is serving tea. On her lap,
one of her cats is purring.
She tells him that once she went to a rare lunch
with a group of students, but I didn't go
because I was saving money.

My father is countering with a story
about the time when he moved
to the house he had just built
and got a new puppy but it died.

He offers to plant some scallions and garlic
in her garden, and graft some plum trees.
Karen blushes slightly, smiles,
and confesses she makes really good
gingerbread cookies that go well with tea.

Each speaks his or her own language,
but it doesn't matter, as Heaven has its own
Center of Simultaneous Translation that works
with headsets without a glitch.

An Empty House

Next summer my mother, my daughter,
and I will go to the house and stay overnight.
We'll borrow a dog from a neighbor and tie it
with a chain in the yard next to the linden tree.
That way nobody will be able to jump
over the locked gate or over the six-foot tall fence.
The dog will bark at every frog
and will keep us awake.

Neighbors will stop by so we'll put
a red ribbon in my daughter's hair
to protect her from the evil eye.
They will bring her pears and hazelnuts
in the lap of their skirts and will tell us
stories to make her laugh.

At night, the bugs will come out
and my daughter will cry
that she doesn't want to sleep there.
A man's aura would strengthen
the foundation of the house, hold up
the beams. He would keep away the ghosts,
build a shield over the illusory
protection of the windows,
prop the door.

We will be scared of sleeping in the house,
will fear the sound of the mice
rambling in the attic, will worry
that drunken men holler at the gate
on their way home from the pub.

That Last Summer

On Monday night a thought woke me up,
got me out of bed in my pajamas in the frost

to dig through the trash in the garage before
I dragged it out to the curb in the morning.

Had to rummage through bags of garbage
till I finally dug them out: butter-colored

sandals with soft soles and ankle straps
I'd worn seven years, took them to a cheap

shop in Romania where I knew the man
wouldn't laugh when I asked him for new soles:

the rotting leather covered inner layers
of desiccated cardboard. I wore these sandals

in all the pictures I took with my father that summer—
we beamed at the camera, not knowing.

My Father's Prayer Book

My father's prayer book smells musty, porous pages
soaking in the dampness of the house. Inside,

he left his finger prints at a children's prayer
everyone knows by heart. The book has prayers

for parents, prayers for daughters, prayers
for the sower and the land, prayers for rain,

for soldiers and enemies, prayers for shepherds,
prayers for travel, prayers for benefactors. Sometimes,

remiss, I don't pick it up for months, its cover
blending into the piles of books on my desk

and guarding the gates of sleepless nights. Some days,
simply the touch or smell of its pages brings him back.

"*Şi-n tot locul mă-nsoţeşte şi de rele mă păzeşte*:
Be with me everywhere and protect me from evil."

LIKE A BURGLAR

As time grows between us, I ransack my mind
for memories of him, like a burglar who is scared at first,

but then, less cautious, turns into the recesses of the room,
looks for money in the armoire first, pushing around

piles of velvet and silk until the unstable shelves collapse
under the heft of heavy clothes unfolding, unfurling.

Like a burglar who looks for money in the usual spots,
under the mattress, tied in a sock or in a handkerchief,

in a hardcover book under the delicate shirts,
and then moves to jewelry hidden in small boxes,

or scavenges for a locked safe, so do I rummage
for memories of my father, like that thief who cases the joint,

knowing someone went to the bank, made a large
withdrawal—lingered in the backroom after lunch.

FOLDING LAUNDRY

While folding laundry, I tuck back
the sleeves of stories my father used to tell.

Neatly arranged on shelves, pink shirts
my daughter is learning to put on by herself,

the drawing facing backwards.
So do I turn inside out a recollection of him,

try it on, see that it doesn't fit,
and I wish I owned a sewing machine to fix it

(there is no problem that buying something
won't fix, but then where do you stash

all the stuff?). Putting away the laundry,
smoothing out the wrinkles, I try to remember

smatterings of words, refrains of his songs,
and wish I had jotted them all down.

Maybe they're written somewhere
inside the folded laundry

and if I rest my hands on top of silk
and velvet, summer will return.

He Inspires Me

He recognizes in me someone else:
he can't have met my father
because they live in different countries

and yet somehow he must know of him,
he must notice his gestures
and posture in my gait.

Words are their own cure: like apples
that heal both sleepiness
and insomnia,

hunger and the sated feeling
of having eaten too much,
words cut the dizzying

effect of sugar with another kind
of sugar—the taste of kindness,
the perfume of patience,

the sound of withholding
advice. Summer is here
and he must have recognized in me

my father,
whose voice rises in church
years afterwards.

Flight Home

Airport Security Check

In line at the gate, a customs officer asks me to interpret
for a seventy-year-old woman who doesn't speak

any English. She gives long answers to the standard
questions: "Have you packed your own bags?"

"Who would help me?" she explains, "my husband
is long gone, and my only daughter lives in America."

I nudge her gently, translating along for the impatient
clerk: "How much money are you bringing with you?"

Embarrassed, at first the woman doesn't understand,
then says her daughter bought her the ticket.

"Have your bags been under your supervision at all times?"
The woman points to her only bag, small and light,

and starts her litany again: "I have only one daughter,
and she left to America thirty years ago."

Preserves

In the deserted house my grandmother's ghost
brings out *dulceață de cireșe amare* in a saucer

from the tea set. Her guests eat it, grateful
that she climbed up on top of a forty-foot-high tree

and picked the cherries, saved them and carefully
took out the pits, wiped the walls where the juice

splattered, measured them, and made jam.
She doesn't know that the house is abandoned.

She doesn't know that someone has left the windows
open and the storm has raged and broken the dishes,

destroyed the old tapestries eaten by mold.
She brings a glass of cold water and entertains

her guests with stories of her youth,
details unexpected like cherry pits in the jar.

THE NEW CHURCH

The old cupola glinted above the clouds, shone
among fir trees, but it took him two hours

to walk all the way up the hill. As he trailed,
the village passed him by, greeted him,

asked about his health, but everybody hurried
to catch the mass, left him leaning against fences,

measuring the road with the walking stick he sculpted.
He yearned for the day when the new church

would be built—right across the road. Now
it rises above the moon: saints in frescoes

meet the eye. The rain has started to cut
through the old shingles on the roof of his empty

house. The apple trees have taken over the sky,
sequestered the gate, sidled over the porch.

Prayer

Thieves are stealing the train tracks,
light signals, and parts of the cars.

Anything metal that can be lifted from a train
is taken away: cables, wires, wheels,

bolts, and screws. The trains that become
a form a prayer, connecting us to the cities

of our beloved, also hook us up with death
with the tracks at the entrance of Bucharest

missing, and the brakes badly repaired.
Protected by the dark, bands of thieves

work together and hide, steal the lines
that help the cities breathe. Trains halt

in the middle of nowhere in the melting heat
to discover that the tracks have disappeared.

Counterfeit Honey

We watched to see if he beat his wife, we frowned
if his kids walked around with dirty clothes,

and we always greeted him first. When we met his wife,
we said, "I kiss your hand," and we took our hats off.

We listened carefully when he spoke because
we wanted to make sure he did not corrupt the honey.

It was so easy to dilute it, lengthen it,
color it, and falsify honey. We held

the glass jar up in the sun and squinted at it,
smacked our lips, and wondered at the miracle

of the new gold. We knew about the cheap
alchemy of added sugar. We prayed that

the magic of bees be left untouched, the grace
preserved, the beekeeper not seduced by money.

THE REPAIRS

A friend gave me a red umbrella with drawings
of a compass. At twenty two, I worked two

jobs to pay for my flight to America, and walking
to my night shift, I held the umbrella's

sturdy handle to protect myself from stray dogs
that howled across a construction site. It never

rained that summer. I kept that umbrella
for twenty years, and when it broke I found a garret

where so many mismatched, ailing gadgets fit.
The old man fixed watches, coffee grinders, glasses' frames.

A God of broken things, he turned and inspected them,
and his hands knew before he did. How he survived

on the coins he charged was not clear—how many
of us cared to repair that umbrella, prayed for rain.

THE COLLECTOR

He collected old parts of TVs that ended up all over
the house, old tubes, and lamps that caught dust.

Even in the mountains people were learning
that you don't repair TVs anymore, nothing

to be done with the new models. Parts sat on desks,
covered the floors of his mother's house and the spare

beds. She was afraid to go to the gate
when people from three villages around stopped by

to inquire about their TVs. She knew too well
how he sometimes took parts from an old one

to repair another, with domino effects that might
include one of her neighbors. One set brought together

a network of stories and quarrels, a holdover
of old times, when we still believed in repairs.

ELDERBERRY SYRUP

One day during communism, when I was fourteen,
our class was pulled out of school and sent on the bus

to the woods at the margin of town to pick elderberry
flowers. They grew wild, spreading out on trees, reaching

to their tops. The woods were still wet with rain
from the day before, the flowers buttery with scent,

the shade bruised with pollen. Having had no notice,
we wore our navy and blue uniforms, our best shoes

sinking into mossy silt. Some of us had always wanted
to use the lavish flowers, discover what they were good for,

what hid behind their beauty. At home, our mothers
made juice out of the flowers, *socată*. The once forbidden

delight of foraging spoiled our pressed uniforms. We
wondered where the poison ended, where healing began.

THE TICKET HOME

When she gave him the last money she had on her,
she felt she could have given him her soul,

then walked away leaving him, a fifteen-year-old,
at the military school in the mountains, where

they woke them up at 5:30 every morning
and made them all run outside for an hour

despite the snow. She didn't realize
it was getting late and she had missed

her regular train. She found herself in the empty
station, and since the express was expensive,

she had to stay overnight. She lay down
on a row of three chairs in the waiting room

and gathered her thin cardigan around her, warmed
by the thought—how tall he had grown, how manly.

Working in Shifts

from ten at night to six in the morning, her sleep
patterns realign themselves like tectonic plates.

She returns in the blue windows of dawn
and learns to nap while the kids try to tiptoe.

When she finally falls into the absurd circle
of her night shift, she has to switch back to morning,

always behind the sleep wave of the others,
always pining, falling asleep standing

while simmering a stew, falling asleep at meetings,
her eyes intensely green, distant music thrumming

in her ears. Leaning, spooled in by a different moon,
her body absorbs the reversed sleep rhythm,

a brackish river forced to flow back from the sea,
seeking the stream's sweetness.

Silk Stockings

At four, we learned to make dresses for our dolls
out of the tops of our mother's thigh-high stockings,

the silk soft and whispery. I remember
the short dresses she wore in the old pictures,

the vivid green, the once trendy polyester.
My sister and I cut off the upper ends of stockings

that shimmered, learned how to thread the needle
through the delicate silk, stitched it so it didn't pull,

gathered it around the chest of the five-inch dolls
an aunt had brought us. We made more outfits,

a cloak with a train, a veil, and learned to treasure scraps
of fabric like our mother who wove a new carpet

out of old clothes she had cut carefully
into a strand then knotted together into blocks of color.

FIFTY CARDIGANS

Stitches tight, rows close to each other,
she knitted our cardigans during long

winters over cold nights, staying up
with insomnia near the blind lamp light

as if our lives depended on them, as if
she made them from stinging nettles,

and we were her wild swans to rescue
from a spell cast under a vow of silence.

That day her daughters-in-law found fifty
cardigans with instructions to give them away.

Friends walked away hugging the soft knit:
she had spun the wool, twisted the skeins

in her serene cabin, miles from the road,
fingers dry with wool-thread keratin.

Our Hands

My grandmother's hands: nails broken
hewing corn, lifting hay.

My father's sandpaper hands: lifting crates
of glass milk bottles onto the truck all night

in a perpetual winter that cracked the skin,
shredded cuticles, callused blisters.

My mother's hands: shriveled,
pruned under water.

She washed clothes for hours and hung them
outside on the line till they froze, then carried

them in to thaw on lukewarm heaters. She brought
the bed sheets inside, so hard to wash

by hand, and our pajamas with their heavenly
smell of ice, fabric folded over like wings.

To Keep Away Wild Boars

To keep away wild boars that filched
the barely ripe corn, they chained a dog

under a tree, poured some water in a clay pot,
and left him little room to walk.

The dog stretched out with hunger and fear,
the chain around his neck chafing his fur,

a collar of raw skin from pulling
when he heard the boars at night. Nobody

around for miles, no houses. A few empty
barns. He whimpered and barked, hills resounding

with distilled dread. Trembling, he sidled up
to the walnut tree, tried to disappear.

He couldn't keep away wild boars;
he couldn't keep away the smell of fright.

WILD MUSHROOMS

Yellow and ripe, red and seductive,
the mushrooms all over my garden

tempt me. I don't trust their round colored
secrets, their gildings and parasols,

their intense wink, the delight of something sprouting
by itself, giving itself away, the absurdity

of their Russian roulette. I wouldn't eat mushrooms
even in my mountains, knowing that my mother

almost died of them when she was twenty.
Although the whole family ate of them,

she alone grew ill. A neighbor collected
bottles of milk for her to drink. It was coming up

all green. Lying in bed, my mother was spinning
in concentric circles of poison, serene.

NOSTALGIA

I tell my mother I want to buy back the house
sold seventeen years ago, where we were born.

Its Mock Orange flowers wash over me, its
apples fill the baskets on the porch, and quinces

ripen in the windows through the winter, light
the rooms. At night, I hear walnuts falling,

hiding among autumn leaves in the smell
of mushrooms, dahlias with heavy heads.

When we visit, the new owners invite us in,
show us the impeccable new bathroom,

and only after letting us gape in awe, tell us
it doesn't really work, they're still using the outhouse,

the boiler won't function till they replace the roof,
and the fence is ready to fall over any day.

SÂNZIENELE

On June 24th girls gather flowers
of Yellow Bedstraw, make small wreaths,

and bring them home. They throw them over
the house, and if the wreath stays on the roof,

they will marry that year. If they place the flowers
under their pillows, they will see in their dreams

the men they will marry. That night,
men don't wander alone for fear of fairies

on the loose. Good fairies (Sânzienele—
whose name comes from Goddess Diana)

are sun deities who bless gardens and people
with their touch. When worshiped with dances

and bonfires, fairies seal the healing power
of medicinal plants and make women fertile.

RUSALIILE

Sometimes fairies steal a young man, and if he speaks
about what happened, he will be paralyzed. They

alter the plants and mar the gardens. Fifty days
after Easter, young men go into the woods to bring

boughs of linden trees with their magical powers
and set them in front of gates, doors, and alleyways.

Dressed in white, the fairies come out at night, and the ground
where they dance burns. Those touched by them are cured

with garlic and wormwood. The linden tree boughs heal
the household and all the ill, keep away the hail

and evil. That's why the night of the Rusalii
you shouldn't walk to a well or sleep under the open sky.

That Sunday, you shouldn't work, wash anything,
climb up trees, start a fight, or travel far.

La Mogoşoaia

At Mogoşoaia, the palace at the edge of Bucharest,
where Constantin Brâncoveanu is celebrated,

that's where we walk to still our worries. The park
spreads for miles, its woods resonant with memories.

In 1714, together with his three sons and his Councilor,
Brâncoveanu was decapitated after he refused

to give up his religion. He watched as his Councilor
was killed first, then his sons one by one,

the youngest last. On the eve of August 16,
the church echoes with the choir singing

on the day when the five saints are remembered.
People stroll, search for respite from heat,

cross the bridge across a pond, reach the chapel,
and listen to the breeze in the walnut trees.

Reading Dante Together

The first time I read *Inferno* I was in the reading room
at the local library with a classmate, balancing

one book between us, struggling with its tercets,
its terza rima. The library owned four copies

of the *Purgatorio*, but only one of the *Inferno*.
We each had our own pace and soon found ourselves

on different pages, failing to speed-read
through layers of footnotes. No Francesca da Rimini

and Paolo who fell in love reading the story of Lancelot
and Guinevere. Our reading together only deepened

our aversion to the sticky room, surrounded by forty people
stuck together in the funneling spirals of required readings

and deadlines. Little did I know I'd be required
to read it twice more, never *Purgatorio* or *Paradiso*.

TUTORING LESSONS

I didn't learn German. The tutor's words I scanned
hypnotized as he arrived every Monday morning

from ten to twelve at my small room in the basement
in Bucharest. We sat at the desk and read out loud

from an expensive edition of *Faust* I had bought
from a street vendor, using half of my scholarship money.

Words, I didn't hear. All I could think of were his lips
and his tongue as he formed the umlaut demonstrating

it to me. Notebooks, I filled out with phrases, idioms,
archaic language from *Faust*. By luck, my thoughts,

he didn't seem to hear. By grace, I held on to the desk
as, unaware, he read the first lines from the dedication:

Again, you show yourselves, you wavering Forms,
Revealed, as you once were, to cloudy vision.

Immigrants' Return

Like a gate in Maramureş, faith welcomes us home
as we are. Some complain that the new houses

look like kitsch palaces, don't fit with the music
of the old church carved out of oak forest.

White porches stand blighted by scaffoldings
for the mansions rising overnight. Following

medieval princes descending with cavalcades
of horses, we return and listen to glinting steeples.

At wells with columns balancing the moon,
we arrive night after night. Some of us are poorer

than when we left. Some of us retrace our steps
in disguised shame. Some of our children

speak a broken language. Some of us see shadows
near fences, silhouettes dissolving in endless sunset.

How Language Subsides

A friend of mine confesses she doesn't
speak Romanian anymore and feels embarrassed

about the remnants of speech. And I wonder
if language recedes like water after a drought,

like the pond we visited in the Adirondacks
where the carp were all lying on their sides

thickening the surface in various forms
of decay, bones exposed, spines bare.

Do words just evaporate like rain?
Do they ebb and subside, leave behind

desiccating fish? In waves, sentence structures
pulse, reflect the shoreline of the soul,

quench its thirst with their undulating
translucence, soothing and blue.

COMFORT

Next to me, someone is speaking and I don't
understand a word. The utter comfort of another

language: no pressure to listen, no obligation
to sympathize, no leaning in. The music

of the speech soothes, and the train purrs.
I am not even sitting on the side with the river view

so I don't follow the seagulls' flight,
don't wonder about the parked cars heaving

under a week's worth of snow. The grace
of a language I don't recognize: nobody wants

anything from me as we travel together
snuggled in a quilt of words, tucked in a silk cocoon,

wrapped in the reassurance of the afternoon,
passengers sleeping in the soft sounds of the train.

Driving on the Bridge

Driving on the bridge, with only one lane each way:
that's how being bilingual feels every day

(well, there is an emergency lane, but it doesn't count).
You have to keep on your side, accomplish more

by settling behind the car in front of you
and ignoring the truck pushing behind you

though from his height he can see there is no place
to go—but maybe that's why he's kissing

your bumper. Somewhere on the right, the river
stretches like a cat, licks its paws, purrs

with the sound of spring. Early May, no smells
sweeter, no trees more generous than

the magnolias on the shore. And yet, all you can do
is focus ahead, learn to trust, and pray.

The Fish

From his training as cabinet maker,
Brâncuşi learned persistence, attention

to detail, love of mathematics. In his studio,
he sculpted his own furniture and welcomed

other artists to the comfort of abstraction.
His pedestals allowed his guests to sit

and breathe, to fly and swim in the sky
and the water of marble. Imagine

eating at his table, the taste of his food,
the meaning of his red wine, the aroma

of polished stone. Stepping into his room
as into a sculpture, livable art, his eye,

the pillow of flight. Imagine the peace
of the fish suspended in the mirror.

BEAUTY AND BLUE

Chagall, Bella in Mourillon

Don't bring me flowers; better, bring me fruit.
Not roses but raspberries, not gladiolas

but apricots. I can focus well next to a plate
of plums, or maybe eat them while I'm reading,

but dahlias unravel me, unlike Chagall's Bella
in Mourillon, who is working next to a vase

of flowers that light up her face like a lamp.
Shadows slide, reflect to a white rhythm

of home and dream. Green lines separate
petals from blue, connect shapes and longing.

The table opens and closes a universe
of yearning and yielding. Hypnosis of pistils,

trance of perfume. She concentrates despite
beauty and blue, enchantment of purple.

Meanwhile, at Her Desk

The marathon runner squeezes his salt,
turns his tibia and fibula into wind chimes.

He churns butter out of stone, sprints holes
in his shoes. He kneads the treadmill,

pulse pounding in his ears, knees screeching,
bewitched. He wakes up at four to run

for two hours before his one-hour commute—
he's trying to beat the train to the City!

On weekend mornings he runs from six
to twelve. More efficient than solar energy,

he could power the house. Meanwhile,
at her desk, the poet writes with arduous

futility: words bob and careen, dart and swirl
under the heft of her implacable enthusiasm.

Unfinished Projects

He claimed the wall was not straight
so he scraped the paint off until he reached

cement. He stopped half way, discovered the corner
was misaligned, took the light fixtures out,

the bulbs and switches, left the bare wires
hanging. The scraping and the dust

covered the furniture and all the detritus
piled in the middle of the room over the carpet

like a sacrificial pyre, clothes and curtains
rumpled up. Likewise, the manuscript I won't

revise lingers and weighs me down, luggage
I carry with me everywhere. Unsettled

in my own house, I turn on the lights,
stick my hands in empty sockets.

SHE WAS SO LAZY

The well next to her house dried up,
filled up with green moss and grasses,

fattened with frogs, the water thickening
like molasses, a syrup of sleepiness.

She smelled—no wonder the word for lazy,
puturoasă, means *stinky*, because nobody

wanted to sit on her couch. She let the front lawn
go to weeds that sprouted flowers

and then seeded the neighbors' yards
despite dirty looks and the triple dose

of Roundup. She threw salt in the corners
of her room to keep away the ants. I hope

they talk that way about me when they find me
writing instead of scrubbing the floors.

Groggy, Revision

refuses to budge, like a hangover on Monday.
Persistent, it fuses to the soul, irascible and gaunt.

Secreted and nauseous, it yearns for a clear eye
and fresh breath. Cantankerous and meddlesome,

it twists with resentment. Pedantic, it finds
fault, counts typos, misses inflections.

Like an old jalopy, it refuses to move, caught
at the intersection between wanting too much

and caring too little. Parts give out one by one
until it takes all your time, it drinks your blood

and comes back to beg, thirsty for more, the seats
crusted over with sweat and burned oil.

Skeptical, the mechanic shakes his head, offers
to take it off your hands for a modest fee.

The Smell of Books

She buys a new book with her lunch money,
chooses a novel instead of the cream-colored

sandals she's wanted for years. Instead of a new
shirt, she buys books with abandon, the way others

attack the sales racks at the mall. Sometimes
she hides the receipts so nobody can see how much

she spends on books, stays up all night reading.
Today she calls me to say she's looking through

her books to give away or take to a used book store
because she is downsizing, dreaming

of building a cabin in the woods. Rummaging
through her shelves, she falls back in her chair,

laughs at the words she wrote in the margins,
discovers that some pages smell like honey.

Doubt

accumulates around the waist, clogs the arteries.
Like lard, it congeals. Like bad doughnuts,

it lingers on the roof of your mouth. Like fried Oreos
that entice you at the fair, but once you buy them

you realize they're burned and brittle, so much sugar
that now they seem sour, steeped in rancid oil

that sogs the paper plate. Like roaches, doubt will invade
your house, roam through cabinets and drawers,

reach their antennae into an opened box
of gourmet crackers, pretend to hesitate.

Like snow, it settles around the front door—
if you don't step out now and then to clear it,

it will clog the eaves, encase the house,
freeze in layers until spring, darkened by silt.

ROMANCE WITH TICKS

Ticks are taking away the joy of walking
barefoot in the grass, of feeling the earth

cast its spell, send its vibrations. Ticks
send macabre messages, use us as a ride,

as hosts to their quenchless thirst. Through blood
transfusions from mice and deer, we become

fuel for ticks' bloated bellies. At night
we check each other's bodies with more care

than in a pornographic dream, touch unreachable
spots, trace the lines of forbidden views,

leave no angles unexplored, the armpits
of secrets, back of the knees, and comb

our fingers through each other's hair. Squinting
in the light, we laugh with an uneasy shudder.

SPRING IN A NEW HOUSE

When the snow thaws, we wait to see which flowers
prove perennials: lavender, bleeding hearts, blue bells.

Which birds twirl in the feeder, sculpt a nest, seal it
with glue. The previous owner left an Adirondack chair

made out of his grandfather's barn in Vermont,
the wood decanting in the rain exposing its long grain.

He left a vise nailed into the work bench; sawdust
trapped in for fifty years, tool box lacquered

smooth as pearls. The couple's gaze cut arches
into doorways, softened window panes, rounded

step stones, fattened the sap of lilac with snails
stuck in branches, trimmed the hydrangea and changed

the tidings of its hues. Every morning, surprise
perennials gift us with letters, relentless, like new love.

QUINCES IN THE HUDSON VALLEY

Apple picking for the third time this fall, only
I am looking for quinces instead. A couple of years

ago I stumbled upon a quince tree in an orchard.
Someone who didn't know what they were tried them,

found them too tart, and dropped them on the ground
with other discarded fruit. Picked them too early

anyway. I should know. In every garden
where we lived we had a quince tree. In spring,

bees bothered the velvet of its flowers. In winter,
we placed the fruit on window sills, and the aroma

filled a space of scarcity and frost. We woke up early
to make a fire, set three large quinces in the oven,

baked them whole on low heat for hours
until the house started to smell like home.

PRAYER TREES

Leaves melt into a smoky smell of walnuts
and mushrooms, the top of trees laced with maps.

Now you can tell apart their magic numbers,
recognize the mathematics of their angles,

the ascetic persistence of their lines,
the steadfastness of roots and seeds.

Prayer trees parallel the balance of your spine
and teach arduous faith, trembling

tenacity. Everyone has a tree to confide in,
glimpses the endless column of its rhythm

and learns that whoever made the obdurate
elasticity of trees can surely alleviate loneliness,

can keep you warm in a snow storm,
allay any ailment, stoke any fire.

A DIFFERENT SENSE OF SPACE

The four of them live in a one-bedroom apartment
with pull-out couch, bunk beds. The kitchen

hardly holds them. Lavish meals fit in the small
refrigerator. Outside the window, a walnut tree fails

to hide gray buildings slumping under peeling paint,
vertigo of ten-storied blocks in Bucharest.

When I return to America, my walls spiral,
stir listless echoes in the empty rooms upstairs.

The space I don't use lingers, languishes,
the same way sometimes I idle away the morning,

looking for some old photograph long lost.
Spare rooms fret, summon more ghosts who scuffle

in the corners. After a few weeks, the house
softens its edges, settles, shrinks.

OUR CHOIR DIRECTOR

Whenever we asked her how she was,
she always redirected back the question,

the way a river can enhance light,
sending waves of gold and silver.

She made us tell our stories, listened,
remembered where we'd been interrupted

a month ago, picking up silk thread
like a master spider. She reveled in music,

lifted her tuning fork to find a note,
sang it softly as if knowing all about

the stridency of self-assertion that mars
the wisdom of a hymn. She evaded

allusions to her plight, smiled, smoothed
down rebel wisps of hair in her wig.

HE SCRIMPS

Maria's husband works abroad in a bakery. With every
loaf of bread, he counts the coins he puts aside.

With every roll, he imagines gifts for his family.
He hasn't been home in three years, although

his colleagues laugh that it would take him
just four hours on the plane. He saves his wages,

not to hoard, but to survive, to alleviate
the hour, one empty afternoon. The only day

he takes off is Monday when everybody else
is at work. After all, his family does not even live

in this country. He might as well work on Saturday
and Sunday, when nobody else wants to. He might

as well reheat leftovers, wear old shoes, go for a walk,
flour sifting a cloud around his clothes.

THE NEW OWNER

The first thing he did after moving into his new house
was take out large clippers and snap off the vines

as if lifting the anchor on a ship. Drained by the long
wait time—closing, packing, moving—he had

imagined himself cutting them for months, the vines
twisted around the trellis and the white pergola

on the patio. Some had knotted themselves through
the fence, and he almost clipped the wire in his assiduous

zeal. Some had split a crevice in the garage wall.
Tenacious, unabashed, only after he was done

and had crammed the cut-off vines into large
trash bags lining on the curb, did he find

the catalogues left by the previous owner:
Concord, Muscadines, Marquis, Neptune, Glenora.

HOME OWNERSHIP RIGHTS

It was the copper-shiny elytra and the rather sweet
stench of the Japanese beetles that made her do it.

She tried at first to shake them off the plants,
but despite the dozens that fell, more came by midday.

Squishing them and leaving the remains out for other
bugs to smell didn't do it either, nor did the traps

that promised to rid the yard of them. Instead,
one morning she set to dig out the forty bushes

of roses that surrounded their new house on all sides:
the Alchemist, the Amazone, Belinda's Dream,

Clytemnestra, Cornelia--didn't leave a single one
standing. Then she called a friend, who drove

in a frenzy and packed her car to the brim
with uprooted roses to replant them.

KEEPSAKES

In her early sixties, the woman willed away
her couches and chairs, outfits and jewels

she imagined one of her daughters-in-law
might like. She spent her last year fixing the house,

trying to avoid the smell of fear. Instead
of asking a friend for a ride to the river,

she hired workers to put in the bay windows
she had always longed for and imagined her son,

the one to whom she left the house, would enjoy. Little
did she know her children would contest the will, ransack

her closets, bundle everything in plastic bags, and rush
to Goodwill, load her antiques in their trucks,

and, under cover of the dark, drive them to the dump,
her perfume seeping from the pores of her house.

TEACHING ROMANIAN TO MY TWO YEAR OLD

She does not repeat words with me in conversation,
does not remember phrases that way. Almost every

word she says comes from a book we read together,
as if every tree in reality is only the image of another

tree from her book. Right now her Romanian world
depends on the pictures in our books. Every

mushroom, bee, caterpillar and fox has its own space,
like the monkey that is playing in the swings in one

of her books merely because the words rhyme:
maimuța se dă huța. She makes me aware of the number

of syllables, conjugations. She pronounces only lines
from books, surprises me every day as if miracles

occur in waves, her second language
skipping behind her, a hopscotch game.

Wanderlust

WRITER IN RESIDENCE AT MAMA TUDURA

I didn't apply to Yaddo.
Instead, I bought a ticket to Romania, went to my mother,
left my three-year old daughter with her for a couple of days
and traveled to the mountains where I was born.
After three hours, I arrived at the house where
my grandmother used to live. No electricity,
no indoor plumbing, no running water.

I spent the day writing and stayed overnight.
My aunt left me a loaf of bread.
At first she said she would stay with me
and asked me if I wanted to go and sleep
in the village, but I didn't.

In the garden, the summer pears were first ripe—
I had to look through the grass to find some fallen.
Some bitter cherries on top of a tree.

I went inside and locked the door,
which kept my aunt's dog from barking.
The dog was tied out in the yard
next to his dish of water, and the ducks moved around,
making a soft noise.

I wanted to go and pick wild mint,
but instead, I wrote. The room
smelled of thyme and rosemary.
Several sets of fences around fences
and the dog would bark if someone were to get close.

In truth, I was afraid,
the way I used to be when we stayed overnight
as a child, years ago.
A bucket of cold water on the mantle,
stories unfolding themselves,
smoked cheese and apples on the shelves.

But Did You Listen to All Those Stories?

All my life I tilled the fields by myself
and nobody helped me. Your grandfather
was always inventing ways to help someone else:
he built houses, ran electricity, fixed power outages,
took pictures, showed films, repaired TVs and radios,
fixed watches, knit cardigans on the machine
for the whole village, patched cauldrons,
built fences, fashioned rat traps,
carved wooden vats for plum brandy,
gave injections to everyone on this side of the mountain—
he was good with his hands like that,

yet not a coin stuck in his pockets. People didn't pay him
with money, or if they did, not one bill have I seen
all these years. They paid him with plum brandy.
Once he brought home a dog someone gave him
in exchange for a piece of land he bartered
(it turned out it was a very good dog).

So I was left with all the work
taking the cows and sheep to the fields,
plowing the land, planting corn and beans,
bringing home the hay and bartering for the large cart,
unloading it all by myself while the water was ready
for the corn mush on the stove. So why do you say

it's hard to write? Did you listen to all those stories
in summer when people came at the gate
to ask for him, but lingered to talk to me,
kept me at the fence, when I should have gone to lie down
for a minute before the cows got hungry
and I had to start it all over again?

MAMA CULIŢA

She washed her hair with lye
she brewed at home by simmering ashes.
She combed her hair in the sun with kerosene from the lamp.
She wove her own skirts, *catrinţe*,
and she bought one new pair of blue tennis shoes
for Easter.

She walked down the road spinning wool:
the drop spindle sang behind her
and danced down to her ankles,
but never slowed down.

She unloaded the horse cart of hay
(her husband was always gone until midnight),
and she plowed the field by herself:
"The only thing men are only good for
is to have their balls crushed between two stones."

She never sat still:
"Do you want Death to find me idle?"
she'd say, in her late eighties,
knitting a wool sock.

She prayed that she'd die in winter
(traded stories about long illnesses,
worried about bed sores in July).
When her husband died in December
the guests at the funeral
were surprised how sprightly she was.

When they left, after she fed the whole village,
she said to her three children who stayed behind to clean:
"I wonder where he went. Go check
to see if he's waiting outside."
She opened the door. The snow was coming down
strong and steady, as if it had held off for her.

THEY GAVE AWAY A TREE

They cut a small tree
that hadn't yet borne fruit,
decorated it with wrapped candy,
apples, walnuts, and lemons,
chocolates with Little Red Riding Hood,
placed the tree in the best room in the house—
casa cea mare—
and called the priest to bless it.

Even the poor gave away
what they could for their souls:
a table with chairs,
a full suit and new shoes
of the right size,

a set of plates and glassware,
wooden spoons,
ceramics, sturdy furniture,
so the receiver could
save them for years and say,
"I got this from Lelea Culiţa
and from Moş Costică;
may their ground be light."

They gave them
when they were still alive,
healthy and thriving.
They gave them to themselves
for the other world.
They gave them to a widower
who placed the decorated tree
on top of a horse cart
and rode back through the village,

someone they knew,
someone in need,
someone to keep their memory near.

THE BELL OF HIS DEEDS

The rich gave to the church
and wrote their own names on labels
printed under an icon, a pew, a chair,
what the family gave or paid for,
the names garish,
a good deed that emptied itself
with telling.

When he helped to build the church,
my grandfather etched his name inside the bell
and they poured metal over it
so nobody could read it,
nobody could tell.

When the bell tolls
before mass,
when a storm steals in,
when an infant is baptized,
when somebody dies,
when a fire breaks out
and everyone rushes to help
with buckets of water, too late,
the bell says his name,
washes away the blame,
decants in the sky
what he did wrong,
what he did right,
and the debates in between.

PLUM ORCHARDS

His excuse was that he had been a prisoner in Russia
for ten years, when his family thought he died,
gave him up, "disappeared." So when he returned home
he said he wasn't going to listen to his wife, work
around the house. He had his way,
did what he wanted.

People forgot his story, but not all the deeds he did for others,
not for his own, not for his wife. He let her take the animals
to pasture, prepare the fields and pick plums
in tall vats to make brandy.

Everybody had orchards of plums as if they couldn't
plant any other fruit trees.
She cursed the plums even as she was gathering them
by buckets, carrying them home in carts she traded for.

She swore at the dozens of liters of brandy they made,
thought they'd use the drink for barter,
pay men to work the fields, lend their horse carts
to bring home hay or wood from the mountains.

In truth, men always found where it was hidden,
brought over friends when the wives were not at home
and before they knew it the gallons all but vanished.
Plum brandy took off the little will power
they still had, controlled the rough land that didn't give
much food but always thrived with plum orchards.

THE TREE

An old man chose a small apple tree from the garden,
cut it low from under the branches
and peeled the bark all around
until it looked white, wet: a light.
The women in the house decorated it
with apples, wrapped candy,
walnuts, lemons, and pretzels.

He carried it through the village
in front of the cart
and listened to the prayers
at several stations on the way:
in front of the house of the departed,
in front of his parents' gate.

When the funeral procession arrived,
the priest and the choir sang.
Colivă blessed and shared,
colaci given away.
He planted a new, fresh tree
on the tomb,

the cemetery turning into an orchard
of plums, black cherries, and apples,
but nobody who came to weed the dahlias
or plant roses
dared to pick the fruit.

AT NIGHT

It rained all night. In the dark, from her window,
she saw a man fall, curse, mumble,
look through the mud
and give up when he figured out that he was holding
horse dung. He left.

She threw the curtain back and went to sleep.
In the morning when the light broke with the roosters,
she opened the gate softly and in the muck on the road
she saw something glitter.

She bent and picked it up:
a full set of teeth.
She washed them at the tap in the yard
and tied them in a handkerchief.

For a week, she made it a habit
to walk. She picked a distaff with wool
and started spinning down the road,
stopping to listen at gates in the evening
when people gathered.

She didn't ask anyone.
She crossed out
the men she knew wouldn't go to the pub
for fear somebody would laugh,
until she detected him.

She didn't talk to him.
In the morning, she put his teeth in a box
and left them at his door,
no crickets, no fireflies, no larks,
no dawn choirs yet.

WE DIDN'T PUT OLD PEOPLE IN NURSING HOMES

If they had no heirs, the elderly often found neighbors
to care for them in old age in an exchange of good will,
but Mr. Ionescu used the system.
He convinced a young couple to support him
and he promised in return to leave them
his house, his property and money, his vineyard.

They cooked stuffed grape leaves for him
and roasted roosters with thyme and celery root,
golden potatoes sloshed in wine, chicken soup,
and trout fresh from the river with tender lines from the grill.
The young woman even took to baking him a loaf of bread
every couple of days. Never did they mumble
that doing laundry, cleaning, and feeding him wasn't right.

Five years later, the old man decided he didn't like them
any more, so he called up his lawyer and had him undo
the papers they had signed. What he didn't say
was that he had found a new young couple
and it started all over again.

DRAGOBETE

February 24

Dragobete is the son of Baba Dochia
from the times of the Dacians.
He likes to run around and kiss girls.
Some say he looks like a goat.
Some say he looks the way
each woman imagines him,
and on this day women
follow the old advice.

Gather snow in a bucket and melt it
to make magic water for the rest of the year.
Collect rain water in vats
and wash your hair with it.
The snow this time of the year
is made out of fairies' smiles,
and if you wash your face with it
you'll become beautiful.

Clean the house
and feed the birds of the sky
because today birds find their mate.
Feed the animals around your house
so you'll have a good year.

Pick snowdrops and violets in the woods
with other young women and men
and when noon comes
run back to the village
so a man you like can try to kiss you
and by the evening
the two of you can announce you are engaged.

How to Make Elderberry Lemonade

Pick elderberry flowers from the deserted garden
the heirs squabbled over and abandoned.

Don't linger to notice that the weeds have outgrown
the trees and the house, have covered the roof.

Don't worry about the walnut tree hit by lightning,
the torn branch half dragging in the grass

and nobody called a neighbor with a saw to cut it.
Don't notice the broken windows,

don't look at the holes in the roof,
where the ceiling has fallen in with the plaster

and part of the wall. Don't step inside the house.
Don't search for turtles and snakes in the yard,

and don't talk to the neighbors to hear their complains
about all the wild animals who have found shelter

in the barn—porcupines and foxes. Don't worry
about all the old pictures yellowing in a chest

of drawers soaked with rain and mold. Somebody else
will pay for a new roof someday. For now, just pick

elderberry flowers from the back of the garden.
At home, place them in a twenty-pound jar,

fill it with water and add four packets of yeast,
three cut lemons, and one pound of sugar.

Tie the top tightly, and in four days the juice
will start to bubble. Don't let it turn to wine.

Drink it when it sparkles and fizzes in your glass,
honey of memory, chime of regret.

NETTLE BATH

When we were kids
we always ran away
from nettles,
knew their sting.

My grandfather said he took baths in nettles:
gathered piles of plants
tall up to his waist,
and spread them in the grass,

got all naked to his underpants
and lay down in nettles,
beat himself with nettles
so they could sting him,

made sure they covered
his whole body
inch by inch,
blister by blister,

welts sprouting
all over his back
and legs, on the inside
of his arms and thighs.

He said bathing in nettles
was good for rheumatism;
I only hope
it was good for something.

THEY WASHED THE BONES WITH WINE

When they dug the grave for the grandfather,
they found the bones of the grandchild,
and they took them out
so the priest could bless them.
They wrapped them in a white cloth bag
and stowed them next to the cross.

One morning, twenty years before,
the mother had found her baby
in the crib at the foot of the bed.
He wasn't breathing.
He was purple and blue.

Now they washed the baby's bones with wine
and put them aside,
then added them back to the tomb
on top of the coffin
as if the grandfather were holding them,

but he was never good with children,
yelled at them, always a gendarme,
even at home, with his own three boys.
How small were the bones?
The baby was two months old.

ONLY THE OLD

In our mountains only old people are left
who can't work the land any more,
so they try to sell it, but nobody's buying.

Those who still raise animals
let them loose on everyone's property
because most people have gone abroad
and there is nobody to watch,
nobody to care.

Strangers pick the apples and pears
from the garden your parents fenced in
and then their dogs attack you under the trees.

It used to be that someone paid to use the land,
but now everyone lets the cows and sheep loose
on your place
and picks all the hazelnuts and plums
as if the land belonged to the whole village.

They know the children are in Bucharest, London,
Rome, and New York,
have scattered abroad, and even the ones who live closer
are trapped by their jobs,
and nobody has the freedom to return.
At a gate, an old woman squints down the road
praying for the silhouette of her son to appear.

SLAUGHTERING THE PIG

For forty days they went vegan, fasting.
The day before Christmas they slaughtered a pig
and the neighbors came to help, held the legs of the pig
while children covered their ears
when they heard the squealing.

Outside, men lit a fire to burn the hair off the skin.
A master with a sharpened knife separated the entrails.
Afterwards, they spent the whole day cutting through
the two hundred pounds, removing the fat from the meat.
A child poured water so a woman
could wash the small and the large intestines.

The house filled with vats of fat. Twenty hours
of preparing the meat, trimming it,
boiling the fat with spices, lining it up in the attic
to smoke, next to sausages, to last all year long.

By the third day, although they had fasted for weeks,
they were all sick of eating *caltaboși,*
cârnați. They moved slowly,
complained after eating sausages at breakfast.
At least they were done with curing all that meat.
Steeped, sloshed in fat, their hearts fluttered.

I Didn't Fight to Keep Them

In the dowry trunk, she had twenty skirts, *catrinţe*:
some she had woven herself; others she received
from her mother. The fashion changed
all the time: glitter stripes of subdued colors
on a black background of pure wool.
The black meant to be slimming,
make her back side small.

She wrapped it all around her waist
and tied a hand-woven seven-foot belt over it,
the front corner pinned up
so she could walk, although it didn't seem
convenient at all, forcing her to take small steps,
prance like a princess.

No seams, the skirt itself looked like a carpet.
After a lifetime of use, old women
used it to carry hay for the calf,
twigs for the fire. In the field, it turned
into a blanket for the children to sit on and play.

During the war, my grandmother
folded carefully her prized skirts
and buried them in a trunk in the garden.
After five years, when she took them out again
the folds had imprinted themselves in the garments,
one side a lighter color than the rest.

I didn't wear them. I didn't hang them
on the walls. I didn't fight to keep them.

Tracing Back the Eyes

My grandfather took pictures of villagers
on that side of the mountain at a time when nobody else

had a camera. After developing them, he kept copies,
drawers full of sepia photographs with scalloped edges.

I wish I could go back to the old house and return them
to the girl who has no other pictures. She is held up

by a mother who looks like a child herself—both smiling
against the background of hand-woven tapestries.

Wrapped in a silk scarf delicate like the wings
of a butterfly, an old woman, now gone for sixty years,

looks familiar, as if I should know seven
of her great-grandchildren, spot them passing by.

Who remembers, who traces back the lines
of genealogy, who recognizes one's own eyes?

School

She held my cheek with one hand
and slapped me with the other, her wedding band
leaving a welt on my face,
and somehow the teacher found the strength to keep it up
for the whole class of thirty students in sixth grade.

In seventh grade, she came with a stick
and hit our bottom, taking turns with everyone in the class.

One student stepped aside from the desk
and tried to hold out his hand—
he got the full sting of the stick
and couldn't write for a couple of days.
By now, most girls had filled out their uniforms
and cringed with embarrassment:
dust was coming out of navy-blue jumpers—
some girls were carefully folding the hems at home
stitching them back to show off their legs
splendid in nylons from the black market.

But nothing compared to Mr. Ionescu's class:
he instructed every student to recite a poem by heart
and then he asked those who hesitated or didn't know it
to come up to the blackboard:
he put them in pairs facing one another
and asked them to slap each other.
At first the kids laughed. They brushed
each other's face like a feather
but then it got harder. Louder.

Four pairs stood in front of the class
and we didn't even realize they were all Roma.
They caressed each other's face.
One boy, two years older, who started school later
and had already begun to shave, staggered.
The teacher paired him with another tall boy
and they hit each other through their tears.
They smiled all along, blushing through the pain.

Math Examination

He examined us by the roster,
sent each of us to the chalkboard to solve a new equation.
Doing math standing in front of the whole class
felt like winters that never ended,
cold that made you sweat.

He called all the boys in class Ionică
and said he could quiz them in such a way
so they knew the answer
or so they didn't.
He went through half of the roster in twenty minutes
and gave everybody a 3 when 4 was the failing grade.
The passing 5 was a miracle anyway,
and we all waited our turn.

Books and notebooks were closed.
When my turn came, he asked me something;
I started well but got stuck on a simple fraction
so he asked me to draw a round loaf of bread on the board.

He told me that when I grew up
I was going to sweep the streets in town
and he was going to walk by me and say hi
and ask me if I remembered this day.
I didn't say anything. I was standing,
facing the whole class, and I felt tears welling up in my eyes
but instead I looked at my classmates—
they were watching, frozen, hoping the lecture was long
so their turn wouldn't come—
and I smiled.

The Paradise of Books

for Mircea Dinutz

Even in high school, we knew it wasn't right
that you did not have tenure
and you had to walk between different high schools
all over town. Your bag burst with books
to give to students who received them like food
in the times when the shelves
of the only bookstore in town
were full of red books with glossy pages
and Ceaușescu's portrait on the cover.

You invited us to your house
and showed us Thomas Mann and Virginia Woolf.
The whole apartment was filled with Proust,
lined with shelves stuffed with Marin Preda,
a rare Heinrich Böll we never saw anywhere else
even when old librarians
let us step behind the stacks.

Aeneadum genitrix, hominum divomque voluptas:
in class we looked up Latin words
and tried to glue them back together.
You put lines from *Aeneid* on the board
and taught us the cadence of dactylic hexameter
as you scanned them syllable by syllable,

in a town where a wrong sentence
could send someone to prison,
in a high school where one day
all the students were called to be interviewed
by an officer from the secret police

and nobody knew who called,
nobody knew the snitch,
whose father worked for the secret police,
which teacher was an agent himself,
someone with tenure.

AUGUST HEAT WAVE

At twenty one I traveled across Romania
as an interpreter for two weeks, carrying

only a small duffel bag with extra clothes,
a long skirt with pharaohs that I had sewn myself,

stitched by hand, and a couple of books. I also
brought along a bulging bag my mother gave me.

When the American I translated for
saw it and asked what was inside, I unzipped it

in the parking lot in the secrecy of the open trunk:
twenty pounds of pears my mother had just picked

from our garden. She knew I was going to need them
in that fiery August—hard fruit she said would ripen

in the car during seven hours of driving every day
on roads with no names on the map, no grocery stores.

STUDENT IN BUCHAREST

On the window sill between glass panes I kept
the food my mother sent via the train conductor

and I waited in line to pick up: *cozonac*—sweet
home-made bread, roasted chicken and *chiftele*,

the pungent, garlic-seasoned fried meatballs.
By the end of the week, only chocolate

and bread crumbs remained. The small window
gave on to the top of the old church with its icon

reputed to do wonders. The bell called
for mass, and women covered their heads

so nobody could see them stepping into a church.
I listened to the music from the dozen students

who lived in former storage rooms. Frost
and snow licked the treats on the window sill.

"OH, EGG SUBLIME"

In college in Bucharest, when a dozen of us
lived in former closets in an attic,

only one bathroom all the way down in the basement,
our friend came over for supper with an egg.

She held the raw egg in her hand like a prize,
nesting it. Somebody fried some potatoes.

Somebody else improvised a salad.
When she left for the night she was still

carrying the egg and was humming,
"oh, egg sublime, oh, egg sublime,"

as she walked out. That uncooked egg
travelled back and forth, an embryo

of everything we didn't have
and everything that was already perfect.

AMERICAN ACCENT

As a senior in college I saw *Forrest Gump*
at Scala, the theater two minutes away from Pitar Moş

in Bucharest, during a long break between classes.
I went to see the movie by myself. A young man

came to sit next to me. The accents in the movie
washed over me. I didn't even breathe.

I didn't turn to see what he looked like.
He put a small paper in my hand,

a note folded over in small squares.
I didn't open it until the movie ended

and I walked out before the credits, still in the dark.
Only after I arrived back to my class

did I open the note: it said he wanted
to ask me out. He didn't write his full name.

The film itself took over, flooded me
with its rhythms. When I spoke

in my American Literature course, the teacher
asked me if I had recently traveled to America.

HOW MANY THOUSANDS OF WORDS?

Hanker, desire, crave, covet, long for, yearn:
in fall, when they took us out of class for two months at a time
to pick grapes, I filled one hundred buckets a day
and learned English words I copied in a notebook
then transferred to lists to carry around.

Groove, habit, routine, rut: each word released
the dopamine gates of the brain, each word pungent
like the dozen kinds of grapes we picked,
the distance between the aura of each meaning
like the grapes we tasted: *Muscat Otonel, Căpşunică.*

Grind, rasp, grate, oppress: the list of synonyms,
each word linked to the other the way a couple of us
strayed away from the group and got lost,
always finding our way back in the burned colors
of the vineyards against the sky.

Grovel, fawn, creep, cringe, wallow, humble oneself:
in ninth grade, I spent a year reading *The Portrait of Dorian Gray.*
When I found a new word
I wrote it in my notebook and added minuscule dots
next to the word in the dictionary
every time I looked it up again.

Grudge: stint, dole, withhold: every word
came with its own aroma. A man balanced on top of a truck
inside a large wood basin full of grapes, boots up to his thighs
as he moved in the grapes, splashed, bent to pick up
the bucket I hoisted up to him, and he laughed.

THICK COFFEE LIKE MOLASSES

Bucharest, 1993

I pour coffee in my favorite mug,
but I don't drink it.

The smell alone reminds me
of all the times I walked

from Magazinul Unirea
where the whole neighborhood

had been erased to build
the Palace of the People.

The boulevard was so straight,
the buildings so tall and grotesque,

identical like a nightmare,
that the fifteen minute walk across

a single block made me soar
to the clouds where the cranes

failed to finish ugly
buildings started ten years before.

I was flying in the sky
like the bride in Chagall

only from each angle I could see
the palace with its gloom.

The mother of the child I tutored
made a coffee so strong

that even the Palace of the People
took off, out of the roots of the hill

with its bunkers and seven stories,
hundreds of rooms for ceremonies,

with its secret catacombs
and underground colonies of fear.

CONTROL BY UTILITIES
Bucharest, 1990

The gray building stoops slightly, paint peeling off,
a crane—eleven stories high—hooked up to the side

since the construction began in 1965. Cracks visible,
painful, like a broken tooth. Seven different units

in a row, slight spaces in between. Even more threatening
with the thought of earthquakes. Because there are no meters

for heat, gas, or water, no trash collection fees,
utilities are paid according to the number of people living

in each apartment, so someone is always watching
to see if a grandchild stays overnight (babies require

the most hot water, you know), or a man dares
to spend the night. A self-appointed watchman

squints at a young woman, inquires who her visitor
might be, questions when exactly he plans to leave.

LIKE FATE

She planted flowers at the back of her house,
where nobody else could see them. Purple

delphiniums nobody could catch a glimpse of.
The sun loved the dianthus and kissed

the sweet peas. And why did she plant them there?
Everybody had the *casa cea mare*, the room where

nobody lived, that held the best furniture and dishes
never used. There she put the freshly cut

gladiolas on the table, as if welcoming
ethereal guests nobody else could perceive.

Others planted roses at the gate, as if trying
to lure in the promises of passersby. Like fate,

she hid behind the tall fence. Kneeling in the sun,
she grafted roses, mulched dahlias, prayed

TELL ME AGAIN

Tell me again the story you always tell me, Mother,
the story with basil and sage.
Softened by grace, your hands.
Softened by kindness, your hair.
Softened by self-denial, the arch of your back.
The story with chamomile and rosemary,
rose hips and elderberry:
insidious shades of remembering and forgetting
chronic state of waiting
strained work of forgiving.

Tell me again the story you always tell me, Mother,
what happened to the apple trees in front of our house,
the house we sold fifteen years ago,
which I want to buy back
but you say I shouldn't.
I live in a different country now,
like millions of young people who left.
Even you can't afford to go back to that house now,
only three hours away from you.

In London and Rome, Tokyo and New York,
someone is counting her pennies
to buy back the old home.

WHAT THE MOTHER SAID ON THE PHONE TO HER SON

*"Because of the Economic Crisis, Romanians Abroad
Are Sending Less Money Home" (Ziare.com)*

From me, less, and from God, more:
may God give back to you
a hundred times
what you gave me.

May He bless
your children.
Bring them all back
so I can raise them for you

and please tell me
that you're coming home.
Yesterday, I don't know why,
a thought washed over me

that I should bake some
whole-wheat bread,
one of those round loaves
you like so much

because you're coming home
and I made bread
and I opened the gate
and I stood there

until a young man
passed by,
and he didn't blink
he didn't ask why,

just took off his hat
and said,
Bogdaproste,
and he broke off a crust

and started eating it
as he walked away
with the bread under his arm
and I watched him

until a rooster called
and I remembered
I had to put the chickens away
for the night.

Layover at a Busy Hub

My mother is lost in the airport.
She begged for a long layover, and although
we taught her to read the Departures Board,
her plane is not even listed yet, still three hours away,
and she begs a man to explain to her where to go.

She hands him a note her ten-year-old granddaughter
wrote for her: "Please help my grandmother
get home," and solicitous, the man fidgets,
finds the flight number from her ticket
and looks it up. Explains that it's not listed yet

but my mother doesn't understand. She thinks
her flight is lost, she's lost, and she frets,
picks up her bag and heads towards
the information line, where nobody
speaks her language anyway.

GOD, DON'T LET ME DIE IN SPRING

I waited too long.
I should have bought a ticket
across the country and sipped the syllables
from your sentences.

I should have stopped writing,
locked the door to my apartment in Queens
and the neighbor who practiced
piano ad nauseam.

I should have packed
seven books to read on the plane
so I didn't have time to think:
it was spring and every budding tulip

in the city broke through the sidewalks.
A child walked past, eating a mango,
biting into it
without peeling it.

On Steinway, women tried on
flowered twenty-dollar dresses
while men lingered at the liquor store
choosing a sweet rosé.

The Greek diner on the corner
served thirty kinds of olives
and the Eastern European bodega
sold twenty types of smoked sausages,

green tomato pickles cured
in ceiling-high barrels—and linden tea.
And with all your sass, you didn't
fly to the city to see.

MARIE PONSOT HAD SEVEN CHILDREN

The picture shows her
surrounded by four boys and a girl,
most of them captivated
by the keys
of her typewriter.

She rhymed in her poems
because she had to write them in her head.
The inner rhyming and half rhyming
sang praises to her kids as she played
and read with them. How did she
write with seven children,
raising them alone?

Did she write at night?
Did she sleep at all?
Did she nap when the baby was napping?
How did she breathe
the air filled with questions and tantrums:
would he like the blue cup or the green?

Wonder captured and sustained,
poetry listening to their thoughts,
poetry singing in the choir
of complaints and demands
for cheese sandwiches
and diaper changes.

The Ghost of My Dissertation Director

My dissertation director offers
to babysit my daughter and brings
a book on Susan Hale she was working on
to read out loud when the child is bored.
They do watercolors together and Karen
takes out a picture of her five cats.

Later, she rolls up her sleeves
and takes out a recipe for whole-wheat bread.
She knows the recipe by heart—
she was the one who found
more poems by Emily Dickinson.
She doesn't ask where the large bowl is
because she directed my comprehensive exams
so everything I learned she already knows.

In the morning, she lets me sleep in,
hushes the child, comforts her with pancakes
and at night she runs a warm bath
and recites a poem—my daughter
repeats it without blinking.
I mess with sequencing my manuscript,
fight with the futility of writing poems,
struggle with midnight doubts
while she brings to my desk
an invisible cup of tea.

Snow Storm

Learning a new language is like being tucked in bed
listening to a snow storm raging on a Friday night.

You are afraid of driving, and every turn takes you
to the edge of a ravine, a four-wheeler pushing behind you,

its high beams glaring into your mirrors, a plow
inching in, scraping close enough to scratch your tires.

You worry about Cedar Hill, and every articulation
in your body is sprained, from knees to knuckles,

hands tight at ten and two as you drive up the hill
approaching the crossroad that catches you behind

another stuck car and the light changes but you can't
budge. Except that now it's Friday night, homemade bread

cooling on the table. Snow settles heavy and thick
in the driveway, as you drift to dream in your mother tongue.

Wearing Something New

I want to find a new favorite poet
the way one tries a new dress and it fits.

We used to buy one outfit per year,
and that summer my mother bought for me

a blue dress. I wore it on Sunday morning
while eating mulberries. A boy was sitting

up in the tree and he threw a mulberry at me,
which landed right on the front of my dress.

I remember we went to the store with wonder
after days of counting, saving, anticipating

around Easter. Nothing could be returned. Often,
we weren't allowed to try clothes on. Today,

I roam the bookstores with the same yearning
for *a se înnoi*: to wear something new.

A PERILOUS BRIDGE

The only way to savor my own language
is to learn another so I can hear inflections,

declensions, conjugations, and for the first time
become aware of inner steps.

Moving to a new town where nobody speaks
my language, I dote on words

like bridges too frail to hold up
a horse. Once I went to a small village

where there was no way for a family to cross
so they walked on ropes over the creek,

and everything they brought across
they carried on their back. So does

a new language offer a perilous bridge,
and ropes alone hold me up.

WANDERLUST

I eat all day because I'm fasting
I laugh all night because I'm crying

I wait for you because it's summer
and only winter warms my bones

I walk barefoot because I'm rich
I burn my shoes because I'm poor

I yell at you because I love you
I smile because you broke my heart

I give advice because I'm naked
I listen because you don't say much

I wash you because you are clean
I miss you because you are here

I pray because my father left
I preach because I don't want to hear

I feast because you are so stingy
I starve because you are austere

I run because I belong home
I stay because of wanderlust

LONGING

Love:
a bruised strawberry

Envy: finding the perfect snack
while wasting time in front of the TV

Faith: writing by hand
next to the computer

Marriage: you're bringing home ice cream
when I text you a picture of hot strawberry rhubarb pie

Love: you are letting me sleep in
on the time-change Sunday

Promise: you make art
out of the perennial flowers in our garden

Beauty: I fell in love with you
before I knew what you look like

Wisdom: reading a library book in two days
and then buying it so I might underline and write in it

Patience: learning a new language
so I can teach my three-year-old daughter; four words ahead of her

Procrastination:
I can tell you I love you tomorrow

Cheating:
praying in another language

EPITHALAMIUM I

Paradise: you always know
whom I mean when I say you.

Resolutions: all in one:
lift weights.

Coffee: the power hour
of ruining my heart.

Buds: your lips before you say
I do.

Footsteps: I lift you up
on my open palms.

Horses: magic of wilderness,
elegance of you.

Table: I hold onto my side of it
so I don't kiss you.

Fir trees: the smell
after you run seven miles.

Home: I love you
in every room.

Your voice:
velvet, salmon, swords.

Winter: you cut me
with ice.

Shadow: you are always there
when I do good.

Soul: dahlias, carnations,
the taste of faith.

Bed: I read
all night.

EPITHALAMIUM II

Silver: I already love you
with syllable and snow.

Hair: your aura
of luminous carelessness.

Pomegranate:
seeds in my teeth.

Shield: no worries,
my knight arrived tonight.

Your eyes: blades
at another end of the world.

Honey: a bee
has already digested our eternity.

Fountain: I have not lived
in vain.

Orchard: all the souls
that blessed me.

Cinnamon: wound me
and heal me.

Garden: let's sit
and I will listen.

Coat: your arms
always around me.

Wall: you see
me.

White wine:
let me wash your feet.

EPITHALAMIUM III

Navel: your mom already
gave me everything.

Wheat: you make me bread
from scratch.

Hold my hand so I can take you
to the vineyards of my childhood.

Fruit: and every way
this world has loved me.

Kiss away the discontent
of war.

Seal: tell me the truth
and be naked.

A thousand:
you are always enough.

Make haste: our dinner is ready,
our house brimming.

Sunday morning: I write
a thank you letter to your mom.

PRAYER FOR A GARDENIA

Directions warn against overwatering,
or letting the soil dry,
against keeping it in direct light
or temperatures lower than 60 degrees,
against touching the flowers,
        vanilla velvet.

How hard is it to care for a gardenia
and keep it alive? Some gifts
are more discovery than offering,
like the gardenia I adore that doesn't thrive,
arrives with buds that instead of opening
wilt and fall.

And how do I keep you happy,
watch your buds blossom,
perfume filling the house with summer
and longing, the song of aroma,
the art of white petals,
        the taste of sunrise?

Sage and Mint

I potted new sage and two kinds of mint
all together and placed them on my writing desk:

my corner of the kitchen table. When I sat
in my chair I prayed. The first stirrings of a poem

smelled like a crushed leaf of basil,
tasted like sage I chewed on as I muttered

syllables in the dictionary, chased the stress
on each syllable. For *fatigue, nervous exhaustion,*

immune system depletion, poor memory
and concentration. I didn't worry about sage smudging

and the practice of cleansing a room. I imagined
what my grandmothers would talk about,

tea they'd make, stories they'd tell,
secrets they'd laugh about, fears they'd dispel.

Prayer for Bees

The cherry trees and plums we planted did not
bear fruit. Even in the fourth year,
they had flowers but that was it. Stunned silence
in the branches.

The sound of bees did not
warm the spring, did not remind us
what we lost.

I spent the day researching flowers
that brought back bees.
Like listing the names of the living
during mass,
saying out loud the names of the flowers
healed me of restlessness
on rainy days, of ennui,
of avoiding responsibility:

crocus, hyacinth, borage,
calendula, wild lilac, bee balm, cosmos,
echinacea, snapdragon, foxglove, hosta,
zinnia, sedum, aster, witch hazel, goldenrod.

Stooped over flowers in the garden,
I listened and watched for bees,
the way we prayed for rain.
Foiled by all the poisons
people spray on their gardens,
I turned to the miles of lawn,
admired the abandoned plot of the deserted house
on our street, where wild flowers
made a home for bees, courting them back.

BAGS

Sewing grocery bags to replace the thin plastic ones
we get at the store, I remember
that at the funeral
the aunts lost sight of my grandfather
and worried he might be sick.

They found him sprawled on the floor face down
half under a table
pulling out his collection of plastic bags,
which were so rare that people reused them,
couldn't buy them at the store.

He had a bag of bags and was offering them
to the old women who walked from one room to another.
In one room an aunt would chant "Tudurică, Tudurică,"
and in the next room, "where is the cabbage?"
all in the same breath.

The aunts didn't laugh at him,
an old man with no daughters, only sons.
They accepted the plastic bags, opened each of them
and smelled it first. One aunt recounted
the story of picking plums from a tree
in a bag that had been used for frozen fish.

As I am sewing bags for produce, I figure
how many of the flimsy plastic ones I use every year
and try to recapture the image of my grandfather
thirty years ago giving them away,
his wife laid out in the other room.

Love Affair with Salt

My heart has a love affair with salt. I can hear
what its rhythm says. Like a lover,

it calls and flutters, whistles when you pass by,
dreams. As hard as I try to avoid salt

and prepare homemade meals, salt crystalizes
the valves, confuses the chambers,

narrows the veins of self-control. Breath
bounds out of sync. Steeped in song,

my heart finds a new drummer that sets
the beat. Slated to read the horoscope of mint

and sage, it languishes to the tune of the ocean,
listens to the whispers of shells, creates

its own ceremony on the shore. Better
to go without than to overflow.

Shopping for a Bathing Suit at Victoria's Secret

after Paul Cezanne, "Still Life with Skull"

Pears, peaches, and apricots, the orange-red,
the trendy coral now available everywhere

that you see on capris and purses. The soft blush
of the peach somebody has bit into, the hesitancy

of the fruit, the perfect roundness that only
lasts one season. Next to the fruit, the skull,

that reminds you. Today, at Victoria's Secret,
shopping for bathing suits, you ask a woman for help.

A good shrink, she listens to your fears
about vacationing on the beach and helps you find four bikinis,

rummages in a bin for matching string bottoms. You try on
every one of them, the light in the fitting room dark

like the background in Cezanne's painting. Listen to her
and try a hot pink top that she says will show off your tan.

Each bathing suit: frenzied self-loathing. It might be easier
to go to heaven than fit into one of them, the skimpy bit,

the bombshell push-up halter, the high-leg string itsy,
the flirt bandeau, the tassel triangle top. So does the fruit

in the painting look back upon the skull: remember
the blunders of rushing, the dimmer lights in the fitting

room, the edgy stilettoes of the woman who listens
without prodding, but declines your 20% off coupon.

What I Learned from Christine Severson

She worried so much about wearing glasses,
posted pictures on FB with them
that, if anything, showed off her beauty
and I learned that when seeing less
I see more, when I wear my glasses
those who look at me see more
of themselves.

She bought too many books that filled
all her shelves, and I learned to stay up
with a book like a friend that I meet
unexpectedly somewhere in Braşov
in the heart of Transylvania, and we both
decide to postpone our trip in the middle
and stay for seven hours
on a bench at the train station at night
to listen to each other's stories
knowing that we won't see each other
for another decade.

She dressed as if she had just fallen in love
and everything fit her just perfectly
with invisible seams,
and I learned to adore
the eighty-seven-year-old women in church
and admire their palms
like the inside of a pearling shell.

ABUSE

A woman picks green beans, counts them,
weighs them, puts them back, the way

she chooses her friends, measures them,
tests them till they snap. She presses her nail

on pears till the skin gives, leaves a dirty moon
in the meat of the fruit that seems to recede

from touch like the shoulder of a woman
who was hit before, knows the cut of a slap.

She knows the pain of a mango
that has been probed, has turned to bruise,

juice bleeding into the skin. Snug in their crates,
avocadoes have learned to take the abuse,

expect the dissatisfied searching: tight,
not ready for guacamole tonight.

ROMANCE WITH COMPOST

In November, we saved a Saturday for our date:
opened the compost bin and loaded the contents

into buckets. Newspapers, coffee grounds,
orange and apple peels, mango stones,

the remains of the fruits we devour. We watched
with interested disgust the worms, wondered

if all of them should be there. Close to the base,
the compost was a black matter like the curdles

of freshly strained mozzarella, fat and nourishing
for the soil. We spread the compost in the garden

imagining already the tomatoes and kale for next
year. Then my darling turned on the rototiller

and rolled the compost into the dirt: mounds
of half-done reminders of feasts and promises.

ROMANCE WITH LEAVES

We don't bag our leaves and stash them at the curb.
We gather them in waves to save over the winter:

rustle of oranges and reds, coppers of long romantic
walks that sing of bliss, farewell to solitude,

the interweaving of hungry hands finding each other.
In May we first transplant tomatoes and cucumbers,

set the carton from spread out cereal boxes
and old newspapers and then water them.

Over wet paper we layer up the smoldering leaves
half turned. Threshold of music and dance,

ritual of gestures that create sacred spaces.
Sifted through the hourglass of trees,

leaves reverse the rhythm of fall, keep the weeds
down, keep the ground moist, keep us humble.

CAGE

We punch a code to gain access,
and the residents' chairs have pads
we have to code again, or the alarms will sound
when an old woman moves or struggles to get up.

Going to a nursing home for Christmas
to visit family opens our nostrils
to the smell of fear.

Hallways meander
between rooms wide open
to someone who is lying in bed,
sometimes with limbs exposed,
the thermostat cranked up high.

My two-year-old wants to explore
every corridor and I struggle to catch up with her
as I steal a glimpse of eyes who turn to see her
while others look away, more bashful.
In her holiday red dress, she doesn't know yet
or maybe she laughs because she knows more.

Towards the window, we find
an indoor bird sanctuary,
four little birds swinging,
pecking, picking seeds.
A fifth one hides,
watches listlessly, pines.

AN APPETIZER CALLED COUCHES

Like shopping hungry,
I dream of gourmet pretzels,
expensive grisines, sesame flatbreads,
my hands shaking like a pastry junky.

Planning tonight's dinner,
I think about tomorrow's supper,
couldn't imagine the sorrow
of those who say they don't like to cook.

Counting the days until I fly home,
I compose lavish lists of treats:
caramele, gogoşi, sarmale,
covrigi, kiortoş, plăcinte.

I warble words like braise,
malaise for food, mirage with food,
glaze, knead, mince, zest, scald.
Verbs parboiled in aroma

marinated in ginger and garlic,
honey and lime, savory and thyme.
Words like molasses and muffins
brioches and blintzes, frosting and icing,

the haze of researching recipes
for *canapele*—literally means couches
and calls for olive tapenade,
goat cheese, basil, and roasted red peppers.

BATHING YOUR FEET

While my daughter swaddles her doll on the floor,
my mother massages my feet on the couch

and tells me stories. I am half asleep.
She says I should bathe my feet in hot water

with ground horseradish root when I have a cold.
Add a little bag of chamomile tea when I'm tired,

pick some lavender from the garden when I can't
settle down, and soak my feet for ten minutes

to fall asleep. She reminds me she used to
massage my feet with țuică, the home-made

distilled plum brandy from the mountains
when I was feeling dizzy and then she wrapped me up

in blankets for the day. Once, when we were children
we got caught in the storm and walked

behind the sliding horse cart that was loaded with hay.
When we arrived home, my father

gathered large snails and made them
cling to the porch in a race, while my mother

washed our feet in hot water with pickling salt
so scare the cold. I was five, and that fall

we moved to the town, because my father
swore he wasn't going see us walk home

through muddy trails any more. Now
my mother laughs and tells me that when the icicles

at the eaves turn into swords, I should bring
some red wine to a boil, just to the first foam,

add a teaspoon of sugar, three black pepper corns,
and have my husband drink it, while I wash his feet.

BREASTFEEDING DURING A SNOW STORM

The baby is sleeping
with my nipple in her mouth
and every time I try to move she whimpers,
opens her eyes: stares, grabs
my nipple back, grips
as if she had teeth.

Pinned under,
pegged, I'm trapped
in my nest of happiness,
fenced in my garden of heaven,
drowsy on the comfortable couch.
A warming cold cloth on the other breast:
swollen and purple, clogged and blue,
heavy, pulsing with blades and
milk. Red and bursting, hard
and painful. Snow
sifts the pines
on the roof.

MARGINALIA

We didn't have books in my house growing up.
In middle school both my sister and I
bought the same Romanian novel so each of us would have a copy.
It cost 20 *lei*, which could have bought me
32 packs of *eugenii*, the communist cookies
filled with cream.

In college I spent all my money on books:
people sold books on the sidewalks,
on the steps of the subway entry at Piaţa Romană.
I paid 350 *lei* for a German edition of *Faust*;
the books on the street sold for the value
in our soul, as if the vendors knew
how much we cared.

When I came to the States at twenty two I told my mother
I was staying for six months and I left my books
at her place, hundreds of books I had bought,
in Romanian, English, and German,
beautiful editions of Shakespeare and *Mrs. Dalloway*.
For the first seven years
every time I went back to Romania during summer
I carried books in my suitcases,
the plane heavy with John Barth, Thomas Pynchon,
and Alice Munro.
My mother kept asking me
when I was returning home
but she never said I should stop bringing all those books.

After ten years I stopped taking books one way
to Romania, and started bringing Romanian books
back to the States: Monica Pillat, Lucian Blaga, and Tudor Arghezi.
I read them for a month after I came home in Poughkeepsie,

then settled back into English
like a brackish river,
and wrote in my books furiously
as if to prove that they were mine
and get used to the idea that I was staying.

Glossary

"Hiding the I" (page 3)
Eu: I

"Double-Distilled Plum Brandy" (page 9)
Must: must, young wine, grape juice that has started the fermentation process

"Washing Our Hair" (page 10)
Cobiliță: a long piece of wood used to balance two buckets of water on one's shoulder

"For Father Tudor Marin" (page 27)
Babă: old woman
Patrafir: the attire worn by a priest in church

"Linden Tea" (page 33)
Flori de tei: linden flowers

"Snow Storm with Mam Tudura" (page 19)
Suman: wool overcoat

"Pickled Peppers" (page 34)
Ardei gogoșari: a variety of peppers

"In This World, May It Be for Your Soul" (page 56)
"Pe lumea asta să fie de sufletul tău;
pe lumea cealaltă să fie de sufletul lui...
"In this world, may it be for your soul;
in the other world, may it be for my father's soul,"
"Să fie primit": "May it be received."

"Nettles" (page 57)
Olimpiadă: the Olympics, a competition organized in schools for major disciplines, such as Mathematics, in which students advance from local schools to the national and international level.

"Letting Go" (page 60)
Dulceață: preserves

"I Wanted to Comb My Fingers through His Hair" (page 66)
Sarmale: stuffed grape leaves or cabbage leaves

"Horse Chestnuts in Bloom" (page 68)
Șubă: overcoat

"My Father's Prayer Book" (page 73)
"Și-n tot locul mă-nsoțește / și de rele mă păzește": "be with me everywhere / and protect me from evil."

"Preserves" (page 79)
Dulceață de cireșe amare: bitter-cherry preserves

"Elderberry Syrup" (page 83)

Socată: a soft drink made with elderberry flowers

"She Was So Lazy" (page 98)

Puturoasă: lazy (it literally means someone who smells bad.)

"Teaching Romanian to My Two Year Old" (page 107)

Maimuţa se dă huţa: the monkey is playing in the swings.

"Mama Culiţa" (page 113)

Catrinţe: hand-woven skirts, usually made out of wool

"They Gave Away a Tree" (page 114)

Casa cea mare: the best room in the house, saved as the guest room

"The Tree" (page 117)

Colivă: a dish made with boiled wheat berries, walnuts, cocoa, and often decorated with candy; *colivă* is blessed by the priest and served as part of the funeral procession and shared feast.

Colaci: woven loaves of bread or pretzels, which are blessed and given away as part of the funeral procession and shared feast

"Slaughtering the Pig" (page 125)

Caltaboşi, cârnaţi: varieties of sausage

"I Didn't Fight to Keep Them" (page 126)

Catrinţe: hand-woven skirts, usually made out of wool

"Student in Bucharest" (page 132)

Cozonac: sweet bread, usually made for Easter, but also for various other holidays

Chiftele: a variety of fried meat dish made with potato and garlic

"How Many Thousands of Words" (page 134)

Muscat Otonel, Căpşunică: varieties of wine grapes

"Like Fate" (page 137)

Casa cea mare: the best room in the house, saved as the guest room

"What the Mother Said on the Phone to Her Son" (page 138)

Bogdaproste: a Romanian word that comes from Bulgarian, where it means "May God forgive your dead." In Romanian, *Bogdaproste* is a word that Orthodox Christians say when they receive food or gifts given at a funeral feast or for a religious holiday.

"An Appetizer Called Couches" (page 161)

Caramele: caramel candy

Gogoşi: donuts

Sarmale: stuffed grape leaves or cabbage leaves

Covrigi: pastry made into the shape of a pretzel or most often in the shape of a circle, first boiled briefly and then baked

Kiortoş: a pastry common in Romania, which looks like a spiral and is covered in a sugary syrup or walnuts

Plăcinte: pies; most commonly, fried dough filled with cheese; or baked filled pastry.

Canapele: canapé, a type of appetizer made with puff pastry or bread
"Bathing Your Feet" (page 162)

Țuică: a type of brandy usually made out of plums
"Marginalia" (page 164)

*Leu (*singular), *lei* (plural): the Romanian national currency. Recently, it was replaced by *Ron/Roni* but the two words are often used interchangeably.

Eugenii: Romanian cookies, usually with vanilla cream.